POSITIVELY

R.A.W.

(Right Attitude Wins)

A Woman with Balls Creates Her Own Life Gems

SANDRA B. TATE

THE **BALLSY COACH**™.com
HELPING YOU HAVE THE BALLS TO WIN!

TATEWORKS LLC, NEW YORK
www.Tateworks.com
A Work-Life Strategy and Coaching Firm
www.PositivelyRawSelf.com
Where Positive Self-Mastery Eliminates Bullshit

LOVE NOTES

"Sandra B. Tate's *Positively R.A.W.* is the must-read book of the decade for anyone wanting to reinvent their lives, empower their spirit, and achieve beyond their wildest dreams! I consult with Sandra monthly to keep me focused on what matters and to get out of my own way. I strongly advise others to do the same!"

~ Philippe SHOCK Matthews, Host
The Phillipe Matthews Show aka
The *"Oprah of the Internet"*

"As a woman and a business owner it is hard to find that right clique with other women business owners. I was pleasantly surprised and happy when I met Ms. Tate. I instantly knew that I needed her to coach me and help me build my personal brand. She is not only professional in her approach to helping women, she gets down to the deep core of what is really going on. As a person who was raised to not tell all your business out in the street, I can honestly say that she is not only professional but she doesn't repeat your personal struggles to anyone.

"I can honestly say that now since I've known Ms. Tate a few years she is one of my most trusted, dearest friends as well as a sounding board to help me though whatever difficulties that I may be facing. I would tell people to run, don't walk, in Ms. Tate's direction to help you get yourself to the next level of your personal and 'Ballsy' Best."

~ Eula M. Young-Guest, COO
Groit's Roll Film Production & Services, Inc.

"I find Sandra Tate's 'Success PowerTalks' most inspiring and motivational. Here's a young woman who understands the dynamics of how to achieve success and is willing to share this with her audience and readers worldwide."

~ Pauline A Reid, CEO
Corporate Connections

"Sandra is a great motivator, trainer, and speaker. She has definitely transformed my way of thinking and helped me to 'Get Ballsy' and define what's important to me to reclaim my life again."

~ Wanda Figueroa

"We are all faced with challenges at some point and time in our lives, but the beauty is that we have within each of us the ability to overcome adversity, poverty, and circumstances. Sandra Tate is an overcomer and a giver. She is using the purpose within her to bring hope, educate, and help others who may be struggling to focus on the positive, move forward, and overcome. For anyone who does not know of her, it doesn't take long to see that she is encouraging, inspiring, and motivating; a personality to know and a voice to hear. Thank you Philippe Shock Matthews for bringing quality interviews of the best positive leaders and individuals who are making a difference, while educating and inspiring others to move forward."

~ Debra Jewell

"Sandra brings an incredible, infectious energy to her work. Unafraid of being provocative or thought-provoking, she shines a sharp intellect and keen spotlight on the issues that we all need to be thinking about to improve our personal lives, as well as the society we live in."

~ Renita Kalhorn, Peak Performance Strategist
The Flow Factor

"Sandra's story is a benchmark for adults and other children who now share the same experiences of mental and emotional abuse from parents and guardians alike. However, she turned tragedy into triumph by discovering her God-given talents early in life by focusing on both academics and being gutsy to go for after her dreams. But Sandra never plays the victim, only the victor. Her journey needs to be shared with the rest of the world who suffers from the same or even more difficult experiences."

~ Derrick Muhammad

"Thank you so much, Ms. Tate, for your motivating classroom teaching on self-worth in the workplace. Many of us in America are selling ourselves short when it comes to letting our potential employer know how much we need to get paid as a salary. I think that your teachings come at a very good time, and I've realized that 'A job is not the same thing as a career,' as one of your students proclaimed. We need to raise the bar if we are to acclaim our self worth in the work force. Thanks, Sandra, for this information. Keep coaching us all to be successful in all aspects of life. You are truly a wonderful person."

~ Alton Tatum

I dedicate this book to my dear, unconditionally loving, strong, powerful, good, and resilient mother, Cynthia Reid, and father, Bobby N. Tate, whose union ushered life into my existence. More importantly, your absence rendered the greatest loving gift of all—my own self-love and sense of uniqueness in the world.

My greatest supporters*: Alonzo Speight, Teddy Portwine, Kehinde and Amanda Peart (MomV), who continued to be my eyes at times when I couldn't see.*

My sisters*: Pauline Reid (Transitioned), Julie Stanley, Grace Ann Gordon, the Green and Peart Family, Barbara Smith and the MBHS family—the true stars in my eyes.*

My brothers*: Denzil Reid (Uncle), Gene Gray, Mark Giordano, Bill Harris, Alonzo Speight, Markell Lambright, Maurice Grant— the gentle warriors who played important roles then and now.*

My grandmothers*: Ethel Tate and Viola Reid, who have dedicated their lives to nurturing us all.*

My grandfathers*: Lebert Reid and Lester Tate, for knowing exactly why, where, what, when, and how to be there as the men I admire.*

For all those people yet to be mentioned, know that your warm faces, gentle hearts. and unique spirits have greeted my every experience throughout my whole life. In the end, you all have tenderly and supportively touched my inner soul more than you will ever know—I Thank You.

Make a positive difference in someone's life and you can change their destiny for the better. Now, that's a precious gem for all of us.

CONTENTS

FOREWORD

How dare she say that?

Sandra B. Tate boldly says that women can "have the balls" to be powerful and make things happen and still be very feminine. She successfully and tastefully applies that euphemism to all women to unleash the power within them.

This distinctive book is a fabulous antidote for the wrong and limiting thinking of far too many women. Sandra observes that *all* women have tremendous substance and great abilities, but sadly, not enough know how to take full advantage of them.

She tackles the wrong paradigms that keep women stuck and keep them from operating at their full potential. **She shows them how to quickly acquire a strong positive attitude so they can create any kind of life they desire, a life full of diamonds!**

Her book is fun and easy to read while providing a no-holds-barred feast of truths. With a clever play on words, she proves that a woman who is *positively R.A.W. (Right Attitude Wins)* obtains the equivalent of "the balls" necessary to overcome all obstacles and prevail.

Sandra helps women get a vividly clear picture and specific direction of how to maximize their whole being so they can get the balls needed to unleash their true power. With her concepts, you can live life to the max.

She shows you how to change everything around, and quickly. What she teaches will create a powerful person who has the balls to use their innate power.

If you want to achieve more success and true happiness but feel stymied or stuck, this book can help you get unstuck and start creating the success you long for and deserve.

As an internationally recognized success expert, I can say that this book provides a delicious antidote that will give any woman the balls needed so that she may achieve all her core desires.

If these are things you want, then now is the time to read this book.

Jack M. Zufelt
"Mentor To Millions"
Author, #1-bestselling-book, *The DNA of Success*
International Keynote Speaker and Trainer
www.dnaofsuccess.com
www.jackzufeltspeaks.com

LETTER FROM THE AUTHOR
A smile is the light in the window of your soul

- You've achieved countless professional successes by many standards, but your personal life is in the dumps, stuck and going nowhere fast.
- You still feel lost, alone, or trapped in a crowd and present relationships are turning sour and typical.
- Your personal life and work life strategies just seems to be passing you by. You simply feel trapped.
- Your outer world doesn't meet your inner expectations.

DO I UNDERSTAND THE SUCCESSFUL, GOAL-DRIVEN, AND AMBITIOUS ROAD YOU ARE TRAVELING RIGHT NOW?

I Absolutely Do!

Just like you, I have worked as an employee and consultant in top-ranking, yet challenging environments. I've learned to value a thing or two about properly managing my personal life outside the professional arena and aligning what matters most with **who I am**. Your life requires self-centered priorities, lifestyle improvements, self-enhanced roles, and work-life balance, but most importantly, *you*. Beyond the glitz and glamour of your well-earned professional successes, the self-mastery of *you* is still the critical key to your own future and its complete happiness. Every area of your life should ebbs and flows by your increased self-awareness, supportive relationships and your ability to eliminate those things that don't fit who or where you are now.

Don't continue to let your obstacles, fears and the stress of living hold you back. It's time your authentic ballsy self takes control and action now. Do you ask yourself, "Why does my life feel so incomplete with so much of the stuff everyone wants and I have?"

This is great question. Actually, the solution is quite simple. You, my friend, are missing the all-important **S.E.L.F.** factor (Self Elevates Life Forward) and once you truly understand that principle, the world really does come alive for you again. Let me explain the power of a courageous life purpose through the story of me gaining my own **S.E.L.F.** wealth.

When I was a technical trainer and project manager at the Administration for Children Services (ACS) in New York City, I was asked to lead a citywide rollout training initiative. At the end of our first session, I reminded the group that they were required to attend the second session. An older woman approached me as we dismissed and informed me that although she enjoyed the training, she wouldn't be able to attend the second session for personal reasons. She then expounded on the reason: her son had been killed on his birthday seven years earlier and since that time she'd never left her home or talked with anyone on that day. She saw no reason to feel optimistic or to feel good since this tragic incident took her only son away. She'd had a very lonely existence ever since.

I related to this story because at a tender age I left my place of birth, London, England to live in Jamaica. I never had my parents around after that and it was extremely lonely and lacking of the closeness that a loving family shared. I couldn't comprehend the woman's loss, but I would help in any way I could. On instinct, I offered my office number and told her we'd schedule time to do a one-on-one training. I told her I understood and would be happy to work with her.

The next day, as I took attendance for the class, I came across her name, and I shared with the attendees that she had a personal reason for being away. To my surprise, she responded, "No, Ms. Tate. I'm here today!" She stood up and shared that because she'd been so moved by my warmth and understanding the day before, she chose to make a critical change that day and came to the class.

That day, I understood the beginnings of creating my own mastery over self and revealing the true me inside, a new **S.E.L.F.** wealth philosophy was being created minus the "Bullshit". It was with that moment of clarity, I began my own journey to seek out this science of success and share my findings with others. My life mastery coaching services and programs as well as reading this book will offer exactly that: an opportunity to explore your own science of success or **S.E.L.F life mastery foundation.** Building consistent wealth within while creating your personal and overall life's destiny—Priceless.

So what are you waiting for? If you are reading this page then you know that this is an important message and you *do* matter. Most importantly, you need to remember that only *you* and your actions can make yourself happy. Like in my story earlier, this professional had to come to that conclusion to change her situation. Isn't it your mastery of **S.E.L.F.** calling for action? The answer to this and more is closer than you think, and it's time to get started right now because:

Life isn't about *finding* yourself.
Life is about *creating* yourself**.**
Let's create consistent, flawless and solid solutions
that will last a lifetime—*your* lifetime.

INTRODUCTION

The significant problems we face cannot be solved
at the level of thinking that created them.
~ Albert Einstein

I have written this book to introduce you to your happier self, the self you have tucked away for a long time. Admit it. You haven't been yourself lately or the world isn't as friendly as you'd hoped. I know exactly how you feel because I had the same experiences, experiences that led me to create my own world within. Now this book has some of those gems that will serve you well too. Are you ready to create this change?

Do you remember the first time you received the most perfect gift? Someone brought or sent you something you didn't even realize you needed. You were blown away by the gesture because it made your day and you felt pretty special. Well, lately, not a lot of people, including yourself, have gotten gifts that special and it's changing the way we collectively see the world. Unfortunately, it's not changing for the better.

This book is about bringing that specialness back into your home, your work and yourself. It's time to stop feeling disempowered, frustrated, hostile and resentful about the way your life has been turning out lately. It's time to take these negative feelings of fear and turn them in the direction of your true destiny. It's time to turn wasted opportunities into fruitful endeavors—Your Jewels. No Bullshit Allowed is Your Motto!

I believe, once you are willing to make those positive tweaks, your overall direction must change too. Your self-wealth is waiting now. Let's get a smile where a frown now resides. Your problems just met their match. I know that once you understand and use these gems, you will get what success can do to truly balance you. Simply put, you will be living not just merely existing—Simply Priceless!

THE JOURNEY OF SELF-DISCOVERY

Knowing yourself is the beginning of all wisdom.

~Aristotle

CHAPTER 1

ZONED AND LOVING IT

Hi and welcome. It's so nice of you to drop in and spend some time on these pages. Although I have a sneaking suspicion you will not regret the time spent. First, I was wondering if you can help me with a very simple question I've pondered myself? Do you know who you are at your very best? I mean, really know without any hesitation? Ah! You paused there didn't you? Well, it's not a trick question, but one of the most important questions we all should ask ourselves. Unfortunately for most, until some life event pushes us in this direction or we get tired of being tired. We just don't spend time getting deep and dirty in mastering our true selves.

As a life mastery coach and trainer, it dawned on me that before I could help others to live positive, productive, and meaningful lives; I had to reach my own best self, my "nirvana." Looking back, I can honestly say that this critical "Aha!" moment was really an awesome self-empowering process in the making. The very first steps of this awakening I captured in my first article, "Zoned and Loving It! Choosing to Live Your Life Fearlessly." I'll share this amazing event with you in a moment. However, let me tell you about a story about a young lady who, like you, didn't get it right initially in her own life. Here's my abbreviated personal story and the changes I had to make to get here.

I was born in London, England in the 1960s. It was a different time for many who, like both my parents, migrated to England with dreams of starting a new life. My mother and father met, fell for each other, and became young parents soon after. Unfortunately, life was more challenging than they were equipped to understand. Bliss didn't last long, but their fights did, and they fought a lot and it's that chaotic environment which became the norm for me. In addition to being used as a pawn between them, I wasn't sure whose arms I would be torn from in any yelling episode which would most likely turn into another fight. My young life just got even more complicated with my "kidnapping," by my father over a month later my mother and I united. He basically took me from school without my mother's knowledge and that became the final straw she tolerated with him. Soon after, I was taken to Montego Bay, Jamaica to be with my mother's family. I was only seven years old in a strange world with even stranger people. My mother then hastily returned to London for work and I was left to sort it out.

I'll just refer to this period as the "Cinderella Journey." Basically, I was treated like the unwanted guest or, more precisely, the maid to order around. However, the wretched treatment and trauma I experienced did not dampen my spirit entirely. Maybe, just knowing my mother was there for me reassured me that I wasn't alone. It actually did make a difference in my small world. It also, forced me to go inward to find real comfort and love I could trust—My own. It was there that I found my greatest strength and good qualities of kindness, love and positive ways of seeing the world. These emotions I came to trust and rely on heavily when the going got tough. It became my natural state of being and I used positive thinking to get through my darkest hours. This was my earliest gem as I grew up and still works nicely to this day. Know this: any adversity you face will only be temporary, if you let it. True-life benefits will come with time and your greater understanding, so always find the jewel within the experience.

I lived with my mother's extended family, but I wasn't really embraced as part of it. The exceptions to my misery were my warm relationships with my late and very noble, respected grandfather, Lebert Reid, and my dearest and smart uncle, Denzil Reid, his son. These two role models left an indelible and inspiring mark on my life. I don't think they ever knew just how much they truly meant to me. They believed in me and reminded me to never to give up or give in.

I learned very quickly what my place was in the household I shared. Even with straight As in school, it was never good enough. The truth is, I was only taken in because my mother paid dearly for my food and board. For almost ten years, I moved from relative to relative while experiencing some of the worst conditions any child should endure. For instance, in my mother's absence, I was responsible for her son at the age of fifteen while attending high school over fifteen miles away. But, through it all, I always kept an upbeat attitude about my life despite the betrayal, pain, lack of love and loneliness I felt all those early years. I didn't get bitter, but I did get better, smarter, and wiser.

You know what they say "What doesn't kill you makes you stronger." Trust me, it's a much better deal in the long run.

Now, here's the first of many good things I will share with you in this book and you'll start noticing the messages all around you. But first, you must open your inner eye and focus on the positive only: life is beautiful—if you deem it so. That's another key thought I've kept with me all these years from my earliest memories to now, and I never let go of this concept. Life becomes easier by only seeing, believing and sharing those feelings that made me happy. It helped me break the spell of despair, any negativity, any feelings of loss or fear.

In one of my favorite books, *Think and Grow Rich*, Napoleon Hill's idea that "whatever the mind can conceive and believe, the mind can achieve" is incredibly compelling. More precisely, it's just that darn simple.

That's exactly the thought I had that created my **SELF Wealth Philosophy** for life and that created this book to share these personal observations with others. It definitely flies in the face of today's society's ideas of success and wealth being about what material possessions you have versus what the true value within you is worth.

You know, it's funny that, for someone who didn't really have an abundance of love in my life, I have created a way to have it overflowing without exception now. Initially, like so many young kids that bounced around like I did, you long for a place to call home, not just a house. It's this notion that made me truly understand the true meaning of "unconditional love." I decided that since my parents were not around to give me all the love I would need, I had to create my own, and I did. By understanding that I was worthy of being loved from within, even without others saying or showing it, I learned to create and be my very best friend.

Most importantly, I was always kind, respectful, compassionate, loving and supportive of my own thoughts, choices and even mistakes. I understood from quite a young age that being my own "greatest fan" was my greatest confidence booster, and it made me fearless too. I was a leader in my own right because I had my own thoughts and without the imprints of others.

I guess that was the real value of not being imprinted by my parents and some of the negative behaviors I was exposed to then. I read, researched and learned a lot through my own experiences, but always was open and respected others who shared similar values too. I learned to see and tackle adversity with the end in mind, the same way I see the success of any goal I created. You never truly fail because you learn something of value, which is important. If you fail again, you become stronger, wiser, and more confident for it—that's the ballsy way to be. This attitude planted quite early grew in me and now I see it as totally—Priceless!

Adversity forces an individual to see facets of weaknesses and pushes you with persistence to create opportunities to fill that gap.

Now you, my reader, will soon use this book to launch thousands of opportunities to change your life in a ballsy "No More Bullshit" kind of way. It's time to own your truth—fully. You will no longer settle for what drifts your way either, but focused on your own fulfillment and helping others do the same. The ripple effect will be amazing based on focus, attitude and persistence. You will be "Zoned for Success." Most importantly, you will finally create your own life gems, too.

Here's my first article and the starting point of many magical formulas for living an amazing life moving forward:

Perhaps someone asked you, **"How are you doing?"** and for the first time, you just felt like telling them the absolute truth: **"I don't really know!"** The days just do not have that special zip anymore. Did you stop to wonder why?

Like many people, especially professional women living in a stressful busy world today, you may be struggling with the uncertainty of your own life's direction. For instance, when you were younger, you had dreams and aspirations. Where did they all go? Now, with the passing of time, most are just memories.

Think of how many times you have reassured yourself that "Today I'm going to change the way I do things." You try but fall short of your intended goal. You are not alone. This "Ferris wheel existence" doesn't take you anywhere; it's the same ups and downs, but you can't move forward. But what do you do about it? Well, maybe it's time to take a fresh look at your world from a different angle. Maybe it's time to get "zoned." I know, because I finally did, and so can you.

According to Dr. Costas Karageorghis, a lecturer in sport psychology at Brunel University, UK, "Flow State is an optimal psychological experience. It's when you're functioning on auto-pilot, when everything clicks into place and goes right." This study, performed on athletes, gives us an insight into how we can utilize the psyche to optimize performance by examining how the athletes in the study thought and how they felt before a major race.

"It's a deeply pleasurable experience and it's something that's not very often experienced by people. Rather it's something that often represents people's peak experiences in a particular area," Doctor Karageorghis notes. Stop for a moment and recall from your own life when you just knew the decision you were about to make was the right one. You knew it had to be right because you didn't experience the usual fears, anxiety, or doubt. Instead, you experienced an elation to see, without surprise, the anticipated result. The sheer confidence, positive attitude, and dogged diligence drove you to see your desired goal through to fruition.

Simply stated, reprogram your thinking and apply an I-can-do-it attitude to everything you set your mind to achieve and it will be done. Didn't your earlier successes prove that? The successes of so many of the athletes in this study are highlighted by how they are defining, focusing and executing their goals. The results naturally follow. Just stating your goals will never bring them about. It is said that "If you change the way you see things, then the things you see will change."

All the choices you are making suddenly draw the right people, opportunities and events your way effortlessly. This way of viewing things slowly eliminates the usual feelings of fear of failure or success, doubts and anxieties. It replaces them with a "can't fail" attitude. This incredible sense of knowing and awareness lights your path and allows you to make clearer decisions for superior performance for both personal and professional successes.

So how can we create and maintain a state of being "zoned" in our own lives? It begins with changing our own belief system based on fears and limitations. Seeing our life as a jigsaw puzzle, we can allow ourselves to see the big picture first in our minds. If you're familiar with Stephen Covey's *The Seven Habits of Highly Effective People*, you'll know that the second habit is "begin with the end in mind." This is an important first step in solving any issue that may come your way and it creates an objective way of looking at the problem too.

Here's an example that brings this point across more clearly. Picture yourself being eighty years old and standing on top of a high hill or mountaintop in your area. As you take in the beautiful scenery without any obstruction, you notice your dearest friend by your side. He or she asks you questions that cause you to reflect on all your experiences, accomplishments and shared challenges. What would your story be? What events in your life would be the most memorable? What experiences would make your life worthwhile? What in your Bucket List would be completed? These are creative questions that will lead you visually straight to those feelings of having a satisfying life, right? Well, that's what true happiness feels like when you put yourself in the picture.

It's never too late to get a start on such a journey, but you have to commit to changing it one piece at a time. These basic observations may be the start of something spectacular. Only you can decide what steps you take. Remember, you can always choose another path. Remember this: your choices are always limitless.

Your background, ethnicity, culture, religion, socioeconomic status or past experiences don't define you—*you* do.

Here are three helpful reflections to start your own process of finding meaning and focusing on what's important to your complete happiness:

- **Self-Knowledge:** Know you. Are you a stranger to what motivates and moves you through life in a healthy way? Not everyone has the courage to travel within and to seek a self-understanding to get the results they desire. For many, it's quite scary to introspectively dissect yourself and delve deep into what makes you tick. However, to make changes that are self-empowering and get you excited about life, you will have to get real deep in knowing who you really are. So here are a few tips to get you to know yourself better:

    A. Reflect for a moment and write down things you know are "quite terrific" about yourself—likes, dislikes, preferences, hobbies, strengths, fears, desires, and passions. Reflect on these qualities and look how they impact your life in general. By creating a list of your personal attributes which are familiar to you, you are also keeping yourself close to your own identity of who you are. Aligning your professional, personal, social and emotional traits gives you a great reference point and helps you to feel more confident and driven.

B. Now is a great time to take personality and psychological tests. These are other great tools to fill in the gap in knowing yourself even more. The Internet is a great resource to access free online assessments and tests ranging from personality, career and interests to psychological tests and much more. The more you answer the more you will understand how you think, interact with people, make decisions, problem solve and live your life in general. With the right attitude, these will become more interesting and fun too.

C. Knowing yourself better by relating to others' perceptions of you is very insightful. By paying close attention to cues from family, co-workers friends, associates, etc., you will be able to receive great feedback about how you act and are understood by them. Be cautious on balancing both perceptions and deriving a balanced viewpoint of yourself, too.

D. Learn. Learn. Learn more about you in all you do. It's a process that will last a lifetime. Be open to all new insights about yourself and be accepting without judging what makes you tick. See this as a journey which will reward you in the short and long run. If you haven't written a journal, now is the time to get one that fits your style. It will help you track all these great inner discoveries. Continue to quench your thirst by learning more through self-discovery and building your self-awareness. You will create new opportunities that will improve your life beyond your wildest imagination.

2. **You Are Always in Control:** Yes, you are and always will be in control. Know that nothing external can be more

powerful than you knowing this. You have been giving a lot of your power to others because of all those roles you've collected over the years. You have big responsibilities, but a person divided cannot stand. Neither can you if you are continuously stretched to every other whim out there. You need to know your priorities, values and what you are willing to give up to secure them, by consciously selecting yourself to be the key motivator of all your actions and choices; don't expect others to be or do it for you. Think, act and do your part to make it happen. Don't ever let your fears sabotage your true happiness. Refer to your strengths when in doubt and continue to strive for your inner joy to keep you grounded.

The journey of a thousand miles begins with the first step. By taking that first step with this different outlook, you are ensuring a positively different outcome, moving in a better direction. Change is constant, and the only guarantee you have is the choice of creating such a change. Not only are your thoughts, what you say, and what you do critical to your results; they are the surest way of making things happen.

It worked for me! Now, isn't it time you tried something new and different? It might be time for you to finally get "Zoned!"

I was convinced after writing this article that to truly change my destiny, I had to dig deep inside and strip all my layers to my core. What I discovered on this journey has shaped my world and myself into this beautiful, confident and quite ballsy life coach and professional woman that I am today. I had to take the first step and the necessary actions to unearth the gems within. I now know who I am without any reservations. It's now your turn to peel away the layers and see and know who you really are deep inside.

Don't have what you need to make you happy?

Create it.

SANDRA'S LIFE GEMS

- Like a book sitting on your library's top shelf, it is great to have it there, but the benefits if not implemented will remain there on the shelf and be no good to anyone. The critical key I learned is the ACTION(S) taken to gain the required results.

- Getting "Zoned" takes a honest assessment of what isn't working and requires us to put the emphasis on self-introspection to implement focus on what needs to be reprogrammed, replaced, improved or eliminated. Just take all "Stress and Bullshit" out of the equation – Period.

- You must start with the end in mind, and that's where you need to jump in or off from. Slowly, your feelings of fear, doubt and anxiety will give way to feelings of fulfillment, satisfaction and superior performances.

- By knowing yourself, you gain the upper hand in seeing weaknesses become less threatening and can then lead with your strengths to gain the upper hand in your life's quest.

CHAPTER 2

DISCOVERING YOUR PURPOSE

Lately, more and more people are coming to the realization that life must mean something more than the stress, bullshit and daily grind, but what? I'm sure, like me, you've given it some thought. Maybe long enough to turn the fish fillet over and settle in, recovering from another hectic day from work. However, I have discovered that these thoughts will purposefully continue to percolate in your subconscious until you give them the full attention they deserve. What can I say? They are persistent.

Don't get me wrong. There will be days when you really feel completely satisfied and productive and that your time has been well spent. It's a great feeling, but it's never consistent enough, and like a rollercoaster, you will be up and then down again. It's those times, when you feel disempowered and the least satisfied that these nagging thoughts are the loudest. Thoughts like "What is it all for?" Or maybe it's that feeling of a higher calling, a calling you are not being faithful to hear. Or it can be a thought that's pretty basic: "What the heck am I supposed to be doing with my life already?"

Like you, I pondered the deeper philosophical meaning to life—more acutely when it came to my own. I wanted to find that elixir that would fill the gap on my own life tracks. However, it wasn't until a particular relationship ended that I made a conscious decision to give myself my own gift of time and space to focus totally on my own complete happiness for a change. So I decided to turn my attention inward again like when I was a child. To truly get to know who I was began with stripping away those erroneous perceptions. Replacing and creating the truth to an everlasting relationship needed clarity, focus, and awareness to move forward. It was only then could I gain the insight to a rather unique mastery or "self first" philosophy.

This was never based on a selfish concept but rather allowing an individual to practice an inner balance, of sorts. This concept allowed me to build a solid foundation for creating a self-wealth-generating mindset and habits that would serve me well consistently. In addition to committing to lifelong learning, building on goals that matched my interests and passions, making those short-term sacrifices for long-term gain and all those opportunities that came rushing in with them. I was able to specifically capture them more clearly by calculating the risks worth taking and those that weren't. I must tell you, I have been happily using this formula ever since. My elixir works and I couldn't be happier.

The first step to believing that your life can be the way you desire it begins with you "Knowing" it can. Right now is the perfect time for me to share something riveting and profound. Back in January, 2011 a book of personal stories of the most common regrets were made public by a palliative Australian nurse, Bonnie Ware. She counseled the dying in their last days. The wisdom shared is priceless and very inspiring too. The stories fit perfectly into my own observations about living one's life before dying.

In the article "Top Five Regrets of the Dying," written by Susie Steiner of *The Guardian,* is an overview of the book of the same name. Simply put, this is a gift that I hope you will take the time to read, learn, and ideas you'll nurture within yourself. I wouldn't be jealous if you stop reading this book and clicked on the link below.

Don't worry, *Positively R.A.W (Right Attitude Wins)* can hold its own and be even more enticing—perfect together. (http://www.guardian.co.uk/lifeandstyle/2012/feb/01/top-five-regrets-of-the-dying)

So how can I help you do the same by turning your life around and making it finally work for you? Well, if you are like so many of my clients, you are not alone nor do you have to stay stuck in a rut either.

※ Traumas, throbbing problems, and pressing issues are only as strong as the power you give them. Choosing to move forward with the best thoughts of the experience or proven solutions while leaving the rest are the keys to personal freedom and ultimate success.

Here are a few observations from my clients about their life's journey while carving out their formula for personal success. Some clients had some pretty simple ideas that brought both clarity and helped them move forward.

One told me, "I started seeing myself as priority one in all my decisions. Furthermore, it became an inbuilt bonus while helping my family and friends do the same in their lives." Another client "continued to create opportunities and solutions by learning more" about herself and "positively applying those principles to goals that felt right."

Yet another client wanted to break away from playing it safe all the time and be more "Open, compassionate and daring about living" her life by her "own rules for a change. Be more comfortable in her own skin and learning to finally to say 'Yes' to life your desires too."

These clients wanted what we all do—to be happier with who we are, to continuously reach our dreams and be excited with our purpose for living. A sort of "inner-knowing" or "self connoisseur." By any measure, this process helps us gain an insight into what it is to have a meaningful life that include achievements, love, money, children, enjoyment and connection to everything without any limitations. As human beings, we possess this need to know, to create, by embracing an ongoing need to discover more ideas about our world and ourselves in it. We basically want to make sense of it all. It's this, spiritual enlightenment that ties all the above factors together. We keep growing and gaining an insight into a larger picture as to why and how we fit in. It's this definitive purpose, a specific meaning for your life, that enriches your self-knowledge, self-worth, self-expression, clarity and inner peace, resulting in your life being absolutely worthwhile.

So how do you solve this age-old mystery and unearth your life's purpose?

Well, to discover your true purpose in life, you must first remove from your mind all erroneous ideas you've been taught, including those that may say you do not actually have a purpose. Do you know that quote by Confucius: "Every journey starts with a single step"? Well, that's exactly how you need to view uncovering your purpose. It will be revealed slowly as you place one foot in front of the other while following your heart, interests, feelings and the exciting way your life unravels to you. You need to be patient, open and flexible to those experiences that feel good to you.

Your mindset is the foundation for everything you create, do and can achieve.

Six Thoughts for Your Purpose

1. **Clarity Finally Appears:** Which is what happens when your thoughts, actions, and focus stay true to your need to grow towards your purpose. You begin to follow your inner guidance system that leads you inwards for answers you seek and you become more confident with what you feel instead of what you think. You no longer experience the frustrations, uncertainty, and disappointments as much. Your attitude towards certain life choices are changing and you are ready to act on them with more confidence.

2. **You Will Eventually Emerge:** Initially you realize you are not trying to find your purpose, but you are open to those activities you find most appealing in your professional, personal, and social life. You do more of

them, which increases your confidence and your direction becomes much clearer.

3. **Materialize and Become You:** You are experiencing more opportunities through people, events and projects that feel right. A body in motion remains in motion, and the more experiences you have, the more you will do the same. You will accept changes that challenge, create and heighten awareness. You start seeing, feeling and exploring a new you and you are loving it.

4. **Timed to Perfection:** Sure, you feel like life has passed you by because your life hadn't turned out the way you expected. You aren't thinking in a fresh way and that's why you keep getting the same old results. Switch it up a bit and just don't let go of your need for a meaningful life. It will come when you least expect it and it will definitely be worth the wait. Be patient and have faith in you and your good feelings and thoughts.

5. **Right on Point:** How many times have you read stories of people being told they were not good enough for one thing or another? Later they became megastars or legends in their field. Why? Because, like you, they felt in their bones they were born to do something great and no amount of dissuasion from an expert or critic could change their minds. Their attitude, persistence, resistance, and consistent actions created that "can-do" attitude. I'll bet on that horse any day of the week, and so should you!

6. **Great Adventure Continues:** It appears everyone around you is on the road to some destination and you aren't yet! Stop stressing, comparing yourself with others and start thinking of all the possibilities awaiting your dreams. This is not a race to a finish line, but a process or journey to reinvent *you*. Your purpose, like any journey to a place unknown, could be complicated by winding roads and several dead ends or it could be as simple as spreading love and hope to every person you meet in life. Who knows? But isn't that the great part of this mystery?

Some advice: always be present in the moment. By being happy in this moment, you are accepting where you are in life and making the most out of every moment. It's in this relaxed and quiet state lays your truest wisdom. Let it all happen naturally and with time it will come together. Life is like a good soufflé that you actually got right—it will take time, but allow it to move at its own accord after you've given it your best and it will be yours and it will be perfect.

CHAPTER 3

CREATING YOUR MISSION STATEMENT FOR LIFE

Decide upon your major definite purpose in life and then organize all your activities around it.
~ Brian Tracy

I often hear people asking themselves, "What am I supposed to be doing with my life?" and "I feel like I was born to do something different than my current job." Knowing your life's purpose—your reason for being—provides you with the road map to fulfilling your mission.

It also frees you from the need to compare yourself with others, which, in my opinion, is one of the biggest stress factors in our society.

This chapter will teach you how to write your mission statement and create a deliberate focus to move you towards an understanding of your reason for being.

What Is a Personal Mission Statement?

Creating a successful life is a very personal choice without any mediocrity. However, creating a plan to get there is an individual process. A Personal Mission Statement is an individual statement that outlines what you want to be (character), what you want to do (achievements and contributions), and the values or principles which your being and doing will be based on. As outlined in Steven Covey's *The Seven Habits of Highly Effective People*, the point is to change habits that are holding you back to those that push you forward to what you desire in life.

To make solid changes requires the **self-knowledge** mentioned earlier: that deep introspection, self-analysis, and writing it down in a journal, that gives you a solid foundation. Writing always helps to clarify those thoughts within and the feelings you need to articulate outward. Another aspect that is vital is **decision making** within a personal mission statement, which will focus and clarify your roadmap to meet your long-term and short-term decisions. It's an excellent point of reference throughout your life and the understanding will magnify your growth and build self-wealth to higher levels in your life.

So, this is what a personal mission statement provides you with: the blueprint for mastery of self and your future success.

Here's a quick and easy exercise for you to do right now. There is no time like the present. Go get a blank sheet of paper, pen and find a quiet, well-lit area to relax in. I would also suggest you do this with a cup of chamomile tea; that always got me relaxed. Now write the following four questions:

- **Who do I want to be?**
- **What do I want to do?**
- **Why do I want to do it?**
- **What do I value most about it?**

This mission of intent allows you to broaden your perspective, explore your deepest thoughts and feelings, and help you clarify your life's purpose and what is really important to you.

Your Mission Statement at Work

Having a mission statement can also help you make better decisions at work. In fact, it is the best career insurance you can have, because once you know why you're here, then your job(s) become only a means toward your mission. Your mission statement also helps you visualize the type of work that best allows you to fulfil your mission in a work setting.

How to Write Your Mission Statement

A mission statement should be no longer than one concise and simple sentence. Great achievers have laser-like focus. Craft your mission statement around a core value (e.g., truth, freedom, inner peace, honor, simplicity, charity, justice, loyalty, kindness, love, optimism, tolerance, etc.).

To narrow down your best mission statement, ask yourself the following powerful questions that will help you visualize what you want your life to look like:

- What do others say you are good at?
- Who is living the life you most desire?
- How do you enjoy expressing your talents?
- If you didn't have to work for a living, what would you do with your time? If you knew you could not fail, what would you be doing?
- What does the ideal world look and feel like to you?

And now, look at your answers and try to combine them so they define your life purpose and act as your personal statement.

How Do You Know You Are Living According to Your Purpose?

You are born with an inner emotional guidance system that tells you when you are in or out of alignment with your life's purpose, based on how you feel. Feelings are strong indicators that reflect the amount of joy you are experiencing.

When you feel joy, passion, enthusiasm, hope and gratitude, you are in perfect sync with your mission. When you discover your purpose, you will find it's something you're amazingly passionate about and want to see fulfilled in this lifetime.

Sometimes, finding your purpose and writing your personal mission statement may take more time, effort and introspection, but like everything you do, follow your heart. This, like so many life strategies, takes practice and rewrites to get just right. Don't rush the process—embrace it. Always back up everything you do with a feeling of appreciation and gratitude. It opens you up to receive divine guidance and a sense of connection without limitation.

Self-Mastery – Bullshit = Your Happiness & Success in Life

SANDRA'S LIFE GEMS

- Creating a life purpose is not a random event. There are series of deep desires that continue to evolve within you. It's not only your responsibility to live your life to the fullest. It's your given right to be happy.

- See your life mission as a series of shopping expeditions. Ladies who love bags, shoes, or trendy outfits do their homework and zero in on a specific store to purchase. Without any purpose or plan, your mall trip is filled with uncovering new ideas for the next adventure. You are always choosing.

- Explore your values and write down the top three that spark your desires. Create a sentence with these ideas to be the mantra for living your best life. What values spark your fire for living?

- What is your intentional statement for living your life? Are you to be laser-focused or a random shopper in all you do? In the end, how you spend your life is as important as why you are you.

CHAPTER 4

THE ART OF TURNING MISFORTUNES INTO JEWELS

When life hands you lemons, you make lemonade.
~ Old proverb

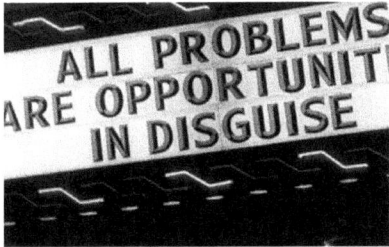

This old saying has long served as a beacon of hope and comfort to those who made mistakes or got pulled under along the way. Let's face it, misfortunes are unavoidable. They are part of life. We all make poor choices and experience their outcomes.

But, like turning lemons into lemonade or precious jewels, we can either learn from our misfortunes and make the most of them, or we can hide our heads in the sand and pretend they don't exist.

The following aims to help you change your attitude towards misfortunes and create a way of turning them into opportunities.

The Difference Lies in the Response to Failure

Probably the single major difference between top achievers and average people lies in their perception of and response to failure. If you want a different outcome, you need to look at failure differently. We are experts in isolating events in our lives and labeling them as failures. What we need to do is see them in the context of the bigger picture. The moment you do that, it'll become obvious that:

- failure is not an event, but a process, just as success is a journey and not a destination,
- failure is not the enemy—it is "fertilizer" that nurtures new vantage points in one's life, and
- failure is temporary like every other state—it is simply a price you pay to achieve success and reach your goals.

Top achievers see failures as isolated incidents and keep their best expectations realistic. Most importantly, they only focus on their strengths and use their power to take as many shots as necessary until something works for them.

Failing Forward

I'd like to introduce you to a great book about failure and the art of moving forward. The author, John C. Maxwell, is America's expert on leadership and founder of the INJOY Group, an organization dedicated to helping people maximize their personal and leadership potential. *Failing Forward: Turning Mistakes into Stepping Stones for Success* is a book that explores stories of folks, like you failing to success. He reveals how all kinds of failures we make in life can become stepping-stones to success in the end. First, we must see that there are valuable lessons to attain from the worst of times. Only when we become comfortable with that reality can we reap the benefits, confidence, and strength to plow through in life.

Mr. Maxwell talks about the main reasons people fail and how to overcome fear instead of being mastered by it. Packed with resourceful suggestions and real-life stories, *Failing Forward* is a powerful guide that will help you move beyond failures and hit your full potential again and again.

The two major steps of failing forward are:

❀ Creating a system that turns mistakes into stepping stones for success

❀ Creating simple ways to increase performance effectiveness

Change Your Response to Failure

Approach failure logically and find out what went wrong. The first step in changing your response to failure is to accept responsibility for your own actions and their outcomes. Gain more insights by asking the right questions, planning your future actions and eliminating limiting beliefs.

Get rid of your negative thinking by looking at an area of your life where you have repeatedly failed and:

❀ Examine your expectations for that area

❀ Adjust your expectations to make them more realistic

❀ Find new ways to do your work

❀ Focus on your strengths and see how you can use them to boost your efforts

Remember, no matter what happens *to* you, what matters is what happens *in* you. In other words, no one can dictate your attitude. Get your act together and hit your full potential because it's what you do after you get back up from Ground Zero that matters.

Buckle up and face your new goals, knowing you will be making mistakes along the way, but getting closer to seeing the jewels in your experiences and inching closer to your dreams through self-mastery.

SANDRA'S LIFE GEMS

🎴 Have you ever thought that misfortune is a gift? Within you is the compass. Tune in to how you feel and the answer will be revealed. Are you open to it?

🎴 Imagine your life with only green lights ahead day in and day out! Everything going your way doesn't help you grow or stand out. Actually, it only helps you fade out.

🎴 Overcome your fear of change by mastering it from the inside out.

🎴 Most people are afraid of introspection, but the strangest thing is that the more you understand your strengths, weakness and overall threats to your true happiness, the more control you have to do something about them.

🎴 Remember this: It is not what happens to you that is really important. It is what happens within you that makes all the difference about a given experience. The value stays positive when it keeps you moving forward.

CHAPTER 5

HOW TO DRAW THE STRAIGHT LINE TO YOUR SUCCESS

*People rarely succeed unless they have fun in what
they are doing.*
~ Dale Carnegie

I've discovered through a lot of reading (and even doing extensive research while writing this book) a very interesting series of observations about true success, love and optimism: happy people seem to be more successful in accomplishing whatever goals they set for themselves in life.

Even if they don't have a clue of what to do or how to do it, they will continue to research and find tools that will help them—a book, informational resource, people, videos or groups online. They will somehow figure it out. They enjoy what they do and it shows as one important factor when looking at your own problem. I saw the same pattern when I decided to create a goal for 2010 and I had a horrible year in my personal and professional life. I knew that for me to change things I had to start with understanding the big picture. In addition to my own attitude and behavior that created the result in the first place. Like preparing for a new recipe in your kitchen, getting the right ingredients, cooking utensils and tools are important. So is having the right resources around you, to make the necessary results work.

Many of us look for success strategies in other people's stories—and there's nothing wrong with that as long as you are gaining from their experiences. You should feel fired up and excited every time you read their tales of woe and triumph. More importantly, how the individual mustered the courage to forge ahead despite all their obstacles, pain and setbacks are examples that strengthen your own resolve. In addition to feeling motivated, following the advice or trying to copy his or her approach towards certain things in life can actually give you a better perspective on how you are coping and moving forward with the issues in yours.

You are a witness to the results and you can analyze those changes in your role model's own understanding and progress. In turn, this observation makes you more aware of your own changes and gives you an effective edge in the world. If you do experience identical problems, then you have a fresh perspective and approach in what was shared and how likely it will apply to your life. You add what you learn to your self-knowledge and your confidence will soar to greater levels. Right here, you are continuously eliminating stress while boosting your confidence with practice. No bullshit there.

Role Models—Do They Help?

Yes. Role models offer incredible benefits to those who are looking for the right kind of advice, motivation and life strategies to overcome their own obstacles. You do not have to reinvent the wheel: just gather the insights gained from strategies used by others. You can then customize them to suit your own situation by knowing your own strengths and weaknesses and tweaking accordingly.

One such person I've admired over the years is Robert Toru Kiyosaki, a fourth-generation Japanese American investor, self-help author, motivational speaker, financial literacy activist and financial commentator. Mr. Kiyosaki is well known for his *Rich Dad, Poor Dad* series of motivational books and other materials, which have sold over 26 million copies. Prior to "making it," Mr. Kiyosaki had experienced bankruptcy, suffered homelessness and lived in the back of a Toyota for several months before starting another business from the ground up.

There's something magnetic about these people that oftentimes makes us forget about where we are and our own struggles, struggles that pale in comparison. At the right time, these stories inspire us to move forward and not give up. At other times, when you feel the lowest, you become more bitter and frustrated. These stories will serve more as an annoyance. I'm here to let you know that when you are feeling like that, you have to see why you feel that way and change your attitude quickly. You are even more at risk of sinking further emotionally, physically and mentally because of those negative responses. Dig deeper and be honest about your personal feelings—there lie some of the most important revelations about you. These stories of inspiration should move you to do better, not feel worse. Such sudden emotional swings happen because of two main factors: lack of clarity and fear.

Everyone has days when you get up and you are raring to go. It's easy. You have an agenda and you are pumped up to get your "to do" list done. What makes it so easy? Simple: you have the desire, the clarity, goals and focus to achieve the day's activities without fail. That's what clarity does: it makes your activities mean something because you are:

1. **Positively excited (and that's the right attitude to have).**

2. **You are prepared with a priority list.**

3. **You are acting on it.**

The lack of clarity is the opposite of all these things. You'll find you don't get up with a zest to change the world. You feel stuck, depressed, and unmotivated. You are not excited nor prepared or focused on being successful in anything or with anyone. You are a blob and you know it because you are feeling it. For me, it wasn't a good place and definitely can imagine the same for you too. We've all been there, and it sucks! These emotions indicate negative vibes.

Then we have an emotion called fear which most of us are very familiar with. This emotion is pre-programmed in all animals and is how people instinctually respond to potential danger. Fear is perceived as quite an unpleasant emotion that causes the belief that someone or something is dangerous, like causing pain or a threat. Acronyms for fear include: False Evidence Appearing Real, or False Expectations Appearing Real, or Face Everything and Recover or False Experiences Appearing Real, and Forget Everything and Run! You get the idea here, I'm sure.

In today's world, it appears there's been a rapid increase of events in the media, communities and within our homes that are fueled by fear. The daily deluges of reports of tragic world events are affecting our overall psyche and perception of the world around us. This in turn, increases the competitive values required which increases the mental health crisis within. This is a vicious cycle with devastating results to the individual who doesn't have the means to cope. The increase of self-medication, material over-indulgences, and individual selfishness are more indications of what's so wrong in our world of "Me-Me-Me" Universe. Clearly, This Fuel: Fear brings so much stress, unrest and anxiety which are just the tip of iceberg for many to feel unworthy and feed into this perpetual Bullshit.

If fear is diagnosed and understood, you will find that in small doses it is not always adaptive, but, as when you are giving a public speech, it serves an important purpose—it encourages you to focus on your topic and to avoid making a fool of yourself, for instance. This kind of fear is not only useful for sharpening your mind, but also for keeping you on your toes. However, some other types of fear that are excessive can become quite crippling, causing you to feel like fleeing even if that's not the appropriate behavior. Such extreme cases would be considered anxiety, which causes panic; they are unrealistic and irrational fears. It's critical to become aware of the difference between potential and real threats. Childhood anxiety can negatively impact healthy development and may predispose people to excessive fear in their later lives.

How do you overcome fear?

You can overcome your fears by creating a stress-free environment within by first focusing on the many things to be grateful for in your life, supporting your thoughts, what you say, and actions to build confidence while dealing with any fear. Don't feed your fears; rather, understand why you are experiencing fears and slowly eliminate them by actually facing them. For instance, I once feared riding bikes, but over the years and after many requests to go bike riding, I decided one day just to do it. I got geared up and got on the back of my friend's customized Kawasaki bike and we took off so fast. I was so scared, but through the wheelies, the fast braking and in and out of traffic, I was still holding tight and finally I allowed myself to enjoy the ride. It was one of the most exhilarating experiences I have ever had. I conquered my fear of bikes and riding them.

Think of your fears and how you can slowly chip away at them one event at a time. While building up your confidence, create a stress-free, loving environment daily. Try the use of candles, soft music, and even drinking chamomile tea versus coffee, which will help. You need to calm the nervous system from stress by relaxing your fearful mind. I can't stress this enough: take a rational look at your fears and start doing small things to ease your mind about them. It will make a world of difference.

What Is Success?

A great question, but first let's narrow down a realistic definition of success. Contrary to what many people believe, success is not having what everybody else has. Instead, it is about getting from where you are right now to where you want to be. Success is the accomplishment of an aim or purpose. Simply put, it's achieving your goals, whatever they are.

In order to get somewhere, you need two things: to know where you're going, and a map. In this case, a clear vision of what you want to achieve and a plan. It's really that easy. The reason most people fail in achieving their dreams is because they don't have a crystal-clear image of what they want to accomplish. And because of that, there is no rock-solid vision about what they want, making them easy prey to fear and doubt.

Here are the five steps that are the core players in your success:

1. Clarity

As mentioned before, the first step is clarity. You need to be totally clear and aware of who you desire to be at all times. Let's get real for a moment here. Ask yourself, "How did I get to where I am today? Taking into consideration the totality of your world it might take a little time for this to sink in. A truthful response would most likely put you in the center of your life. Your thoughts, decisions, and actions brought you to this present moment. Well, the good news is that nothing in life is permanent, not even this result. So, the question really is where do you desire to go, be, and learn next? Only you can create the momentum for change and your life's results. How important is changing the way things are to how it should be depends wholly on you. Believe it or not your overall happiness relies on it. Being willing to take charge of your world takes courage, seeing the bigger picture and not fearing whatever is required to get there.

2. The Action Life Plan

Next, you need to plan your actions that will bring you closer and closer to your dreams—otherwise, they'll be just dreams. Create a map that includes everything you'll need to do in order to move forward with consistency and purpose. It's actually pretty simple:

A. What is my destination? A life map is helpful for your future. Look at your past and patterns that help and those that don't. Start with the end in mind and connect the dots forward to the future.

B. How will I get there? Without a purpose, you have no life meaning and that's what makes you feel fulfilled, right? From the earlier chapters you should have a pretty good idea how to create the purpose and then the big dreams.

C. Make short-term goals which will be milestones along your way to your destination. Breaking your long-term plan into short-term goals, you can gauge what feels right to you. That will let you know you are on the right track. Being flexible in any plan will allow you to adjust as conditions change (and they always do).

D. Keep refining and tweaking your process to your destination. It will take longer at points based on your clarity, focus and priority. Have you ever gone on your phone to search on a map? The image starts out quite small and then you zoom in. It becomes clearer and you can apply the specific information to the overall picture, and then you zoom out. Well, that's what tweaking does and you follow through, finding clues to make your destination more certain. Don't get impatient it will all come together in the end.

E. Achieving any goal requires you to market yourself by adding the value you can provide to others and communicating it in every way. You will find, especially when setting career goals, that this impresses others to help you get to your goal. If you know what you want and how to get there, then it's easier for others to help you do just that.

F. The success principles discussed earlier will come in handy to help you identify and maintain the values you believe in.

3. Measure Your Results

You can measure your results using Key Performance Indicators that help you track your progress. There are two types of indicators: measurable and actionable.

For example:

> *Measurable KPI*—How many joint venture deals you do
> *Actionable KPI*—The steps required to make this happen; how many Skype calls you do with potential JV partners.

4. Enforce Self-Discipline

Discipline is the channel through which your entire power must flow towards your goals. The essence of self-discipline is to release specific quantities of power and focus them exactly where needed. It will help you control your emotions, as they are the driving force that puts your decisions into action.

5. Enjoy The Ride!

Success is a journey. Enjoy every step of the way, turn problems into creative challenges, and harness the power of gratitude. Learn to always "pay it forward." This is when someone is requesting the beneficiary of a good deed to repay it to others instead of the original benefactor. This is a rather old concept, but the actual phrase may have been coined by Lily Hardy Hammond in her 1916 book, *In the Garden of Delight*.

In 2000, Catherine Ryan Hyde's novel, *Pay it Forward,* was published and adapted in a Warner Brother's film of the same name. In it, the concept is described as an obligation to do three good deeds for others in response to a good deed that one receives. The condition was that such good deeds should accomplish things that other person couldn't accomplish on their own. In this way, the practice would spread exponentially throughout society. It was clear that the ratio of three to one would soon have such an impact the world over, resulting in making the world a better place and creating a spirit of goodwill.

Give what you want to receive and you won't have to worry about receiving it. Help others succeed and you will have strong advocates that will support you on your path to fulfilling your dreams.

Create a path to your success by using these concepts or one will undoubtedly be created for you.

SANDRA'S LIFE GEMS

- What success is and what it means to you begins the fluid process of manifesting your own complete happiness or peace of mind. Success varies from person to person, from getting what you want in life, to when you triumph over adversity, or to achieving financial independence and prosperity.

- When you feel a little envious of another's success, do a gut check. You will find there is more you can do about the lack of clarity or being fearful in your own life. Grab a notebook and make a commitment to create a S.M.A.R.T Goal (desired outcome). Your goal has to be Specific, Measurable and Achievable, Realistic and Time-bound (state when you hope to achieve it). To cover all important aspects in life, set goals within these categories of key areas of your life: well being, relationship, personal development, fun and creativity, physical environment, finances and career.

- Clarity is like a port to your success. How can you navigate to get there? By asking the right questions, such as "What do I really desire here?" "How will I feel having it?" "What's really holding me back?", you can find your way.

- Let's punch fear in the face right now. What happens if you couldn't fail with the next thing you desired to have? What is your real excuse for not starting that plan now?

- Enforcing self-discipline to achieve your goal is the finishing touch. Consistently edge forward no matter what and finally you can enjoy the fruits of your labor. How sweet it is!

CHAPTER 6

ARE YOUR SUCCESS PRINCIPLES GOOD TO YOU?

Success is not the key to happiness. Happiness is the key to success. If you love what you are doing, you will be successful.
~ Herman Cain, American businessman, author, and speaker

Success comes in many forms and has many definitions, depending on what you are searching for.

But anyone who has ever reached any level of success has followed certain rules that changed their habits and shaped their successful mindset.

If you will consistently apply the following principles to any area of your life, you will experience some amazing levels of success:

1. You Must Take Personal Responsibility for Your Life

Realize that you alone are responsible for everything that is going on in your life right now, including your relationships, your health and fitness, your income, everything. If you don't like your current outcomes, you have two choices: blame external events for your lack of results (e.g., the economy, lack of education, etc.) or simply change the thoughts you think, the images you hold in your mind and the actions you take until you get better results.

2. Find Your Purpose in Life

Without a clear purpose in life, it's easy to get distracted from your journey and achieve little. Know why you're here. There's an old saying: "If you don't know where you're going, you'll end up somewhere else."

With a definite purpose, everything seems to fall into place, and you'll be doing what you love to do. You become magically surrounded with the right people, the best resources and the perfect circumstances to help you act in alignment with your purpose.

3. Decide What You Want

The first step to getting what you want is to decide what you want. Once you have found your true purpose, decide what you want to accomplish and experience. Simply put, what does success look like to you?

One of the main reasons why most people don't get what they want is because they haven't clearly decided what they want. Have a clear picture of what exactly it is you want to achieve or become and hold this image in your mind all the time. Start with the end in mind and stop settling for less than you want.

4. Set SMART Goals

Next, define exactly what you want to accomplish by making it a goal. Your goal has to be Specific, Measurable and Achievable, Realistic and Time-bound (state when you hope to achieve it). To cover all-important aspects in life, set goals within these categories of key areas of your life: wellbeing, relationship, personal development, fun and creativity, physical environment, finances and career.

5. Plan and Take Action

The process of getting from where you are to where you want to be isn't quite like using the GPS in your car. For such plans to really work relies on a system that is as fluid to changes of one's desires, growth and seizing opportunities when they present themselves. Take, for instance, planning a trip to see friends and family in part of the country. For such a cross-country fun road trip to see all your folks, you will need to manage your time and resources in the most efficient way, including planning for detours, emergencies and other changes you didn't even plan.

Success in life works the same way. All you need to do is decide where you want to go by deciding what you want, locking in the destination through goal setting, affirmations, visualization, and moving towards your various goals. Accomplishing one goal and plan at a time is key. Always preparing for changes to any plan will make it easier, just like in life. Be willing and flexible with your life plans and all prioritizations which are based on your needs will stay easy and important to you. Don't forget to have fun with it too.

6. Attitude of Gratitude

Express gratitude and appreciation for all there is in your life right now, as gratitude puts you in a great state of harmony with the universe. Create a mental image of yourself having already achieved your goals and generate the feelings of being successful.

Your mind is your single greatest tool on your path to fulfilling your dreams. And you can harness this amazing power by building the right mindset and attitude to support what it takes to get to your destination. This is the best adventure you could possibly imagine!

SANDRA'S LIFE GEMS

❋ Whose life is it anyway? You are no longer drifting through life blaming everything external that negatively impacted your life. You are free to create your own destiny by taking ownership; you can make things happen *for* you instead of *to* you.

❋ Right attitude and mindset are the keys to your success, or, if you fail, it will be the key to your own demise. Taking personal responsibility takes the results from out there and placing it firmly in your hands where it should be.

❋ You will learn more valuable lessons from failure than any so-called successes. Believe it or not, failures will always teach you what not to do. In the long run that will be more valuable than never experiencing it at all.

❋ If you fail to plan you are definitely planning to fail. The structure is as important as the flexibility to change it. An example of inflexibility is that of creating a personal or business plan and sticking with it despite changes in your environment, just like business plans that are out of date because their business environment is moving so fast and trends are coming and leaving at Mach speeds. Your personal life plan needs to be flexible to afford you the right to change them as your needs grow. Change with change.

❋ By opening your mind to receive all the possibilities, you will be sure to find an option that's best for you.

CHAPTER 7

GOAL-SETTING SECRETS FOR LIFE

When it is obvious that the goals cannot be reached,
don't adjust the goals, adjust the action steps.
~ Confucius

Understanding Goal Setting

- Goal setting is such a powerful way of motivating yourself! It's easy to understand why; it provides tremendous clarity and a sense of purpose.

- Imagine arriving in a large city and being told to drive to a particular home in that city. But there are no road signs and you have no map of the city. In fact, all you have is a very basic description of the home where you need to go.

How long do you think it would take you to find a home in a city without a road map and road signs? The answer is probably forever. If you somehow did find the home, it would be a matter of luck. And shockingly, this is the way most people live their lives.

True Happiness Requires Goals

Earl Nightingale once wrote: *"Happiness is the progressive realization of a worthy ideal or goal."*

In other words, you only feel truly happy when you are moving towards something that is important to you.

Here is a powerful tool I want to introduce you to. It is a unique goal-setting resource designed to complement your daily efforts. It's a goal-setting application called **GoalsOnTrack** and it has worked very well for me. It saves me a lot of time in keeping track of my goals and, most importantly, it helps me better organize my daily to-dos towards achieving my goals.

GoalsOnTrack—Features and Benefits

GoalsOnTrack is a web-based goal-setting app that allows you to set goals, track your progress, manage action steps and use various metrics to keep you focused and updated. The software allows you to easily set SMART goals and forces you to define your goals and state why they are important to you. Big goals can be split into smaller sub-goals, which can then be broken down into tasks.

To help you visualize your goals, you can select a picture to represent each one from a fine selection of motivational photos (or upload your own) and the app will then create an inspiring slideshow that you can play any time you like. It works pretty much like a vision board, which will help you generate the feelings of having already achieved your goals.

This is a powerful tool that helps you stay on track with your goals and vision. So choose your goals wisely and make sure they are 100% aligned with your core values and your life purpose. In the end, this is the ultimate motivation you get: moving towards that which makes you feel passionate, enthusiastic and excited!

You can watch a features tour of GoalsOnTrack on YouTube at this website:

http://www.youtube.com/watch?v=ZXSKGT-U1gI&feature= player_embedded

SANDRA'S LIFE GEMS

- Goal-setting provides clarity and a sense of purpose that is critical to a purposeful life and being happy.
- Your complete happiness requires goals that are progressive with your growth as the person you are meant to be.
- Any tool, book, or reference material provided here or anywhere else online or offline requires one thing—YOU IMPLEMENTING IT! Taking consistent action is necessary to achieve anything, especially your goals.
- Aligning your core values, life purpose and goals will create the yellow brick road to your dreams. You are ensuring a structured, solid foundation to your overall happiness and well-being.
- Remember: ACTION. ACTION. ACTION!

CHAPTER 8

HOW TO BUILD HEALTHY LIFELONG RELATIONSHIPS

Relationships are part of a vast plan for our enlightenment, the Holy Spirit's blueprint by which each individual soul is led to greater awareness and expanded love. Relationships are the Holy Spirit's laboratories in which he brings together people who have the maximal opportunity for mutual growth.

~ Marianne Williamson

What is a healthy relationship anyway? Great question. A healthy relationship is known to be one built on respect, sharing, trust, support and love. Both partners believe that they are equal, and both share in the power and control. These characteristics instill a strong and healthy foundation for relationships and friendships for the most part. People who have satisfying relationships are known to be much happier, have fewer health problems, and live much longer.

Healthy relationships are more fun to be in and make you feel good about yourself. Daily doses of support from family and friends can create wonders in the big and little events.

Why are relationships important in people's lives?

It is easy to feel overwhelmed and pushed aside when life gets tough and you are faced with stressful situations. All you seem to want is to keep a low profile and stay by yourself for a while. But this is exactly when you need your friends' support!

Building meaningful and caring relationships helps you keep a positive outlook and stay away from negative feelings such as anger or despair. Expressing your feelings, concerns, and ideals with the people around you helps you stay connected and maintain a healthy level of support.

Having a close core of friends and family can provide you with perspectives on various thoughts, which may help making subjective decisions that appear too close or complex in nature.

Understanding Healthy Relationships

The first step in understanding healthy and fulfilling relationships is to take people as they are. Everyone has their own set of values, beliefs, and unique experiences, just like you do. So trying to change people is futile. Instead, see each person's value as a gift for you to gain more knowledge of who you are from knowing the person.

To simplify this thought, think of a time you bought a product, say a car. One day you are walking by a used car dealership and there on the lot is this incredible red mustang! (Yes, I know it's your favorite American car.) You envision zooming down the highway with the windows down and your hair blowing in the wind. This car is so made for you. You get jolted back to reality when the salesman interrupts you to ask if you are interested in the car. Of course you are. So there he is, rambling off the car's specifications, mileage, age, and warranty information and so on. One catch: it covers only "as-is" conditions. Do you still ask if they can modify it for a double wishbone suspension? Well, that wouldn't be "as-is," would it?

The point here is that this is like people you meet in your daily life. If you desire their friendship, you have to accept them for who they are—the way they are right now.

While getting to know anyone, get to know their characteristics, values, mental-emotional state and shared ideas about responsibilities. In addition, assess their sense of respect, humor, closeness, support, communication, or affection, among other things.

Rather than trying to make them see things like you do or change their value system, show a little curiosity. Discover why your friends believe what they do and see how their experiences have determined their perspectives.

How do you know that you have a healthy relationship with someone?

You know it because it makes you feel good about yourself every time you are around that person. It results in mental-emotional, social, and physical benefits, as mentioned earlier, characteristics that keep you feeling more complete and loved. On the other hand, unhealthy or negative relationships will emotionally make you feel depressed, degraded, ignored, or isolated. Comments shared are threatening and other relationships are controlled. Extreme cases include being slapped, pushed or punched to make you angry or even scared.

Healthy relationships include a similar amount of give and take, while unhealthy relationships are totally unbalanced. For example, at some point you may start to feel that you are giving the other person all the attention and you're getting nothing in return. This isn't good for you, and you deserve to have the attention you need.

You should also feel safe around the other person and feel that you can open up to them. In a healthy relationship, you love spending time with the other person and communicating your thoughts, instead of feeling forced or obligated to do so.

"I've been accused of vulgarity. I say that's bullshit."
~ Mel Brooks

Letting Go of Unhealthy "*Bullshit*" Relationships

As you go through your life and become more mature and wiser with the years, your core needs will change. Even though your old relationships may give you a certain kind of comfort, they may no longer give you the support you need or desire. This is when you need to either put an end to them or limit the time you invest in a relationship you deem negative or toxic to your life. It's time to own your crappy choices, otherwise, known as the "Bullshit" that needs to be gone—Starting Right Now. Let's explore this and other facets of your life that tend to be rather unhealthy – A steaming pile that just stinks up your life continuously. You can no longer deny it.

If a relationship makes you feel stressed, angry, fearful, unhappy, or depressed constantly, you need to terminate it. Instead, use that energy and time to build new and fruitful relationships that support your dreams, your ideas of true happiness and you. Healthy and fulfilling partnerships are important for your emotional and physical well-being. So it is imperative that you choose your connections wisely and only nurture those friendships that make you feel congruent with your goals and vision.

Let's Talk About the "Dating" Process That Works for You

Now, that we have an idea of what an unhealthy connection feels like, it's time to discuss those that feels just right. For instance, let's look at the classic fairy tale of Goldilocks and the Three Bears. Sure, you remember it with that little girl stumbling into the home of this family of bears in the woods. She proceeded to taste the porridge that was cooling in their absence. She eventually settled for the bowl that was just the right temperature and I guess for her delicate palate. After enjoying it, she made herself at home in one of the beds. Okay, I know you are wondering where is this going is. Okay, okay—I'll tell you. This story runs parallel; believe it or not, to the way we adults in this busy, technologically driven world attempt to find that "special" connection or significant mate.

Here comes the fun part, open wide, and say, "*Ahhhhh!*" Yes, it's the exciting world of exploring the proper way(s) of dating? Clearly, most people who have matured with their twenties, thirties, forties, and fifties are finding that both their expectations and the stage or age will now dictate more of their preferences for the next person. It doesn't take much to realize that each decade brings its own demands and priorities which in turn create the urgency to meet certain goals.

To not belabor the stages, let's just say the twenties will bring more self-discovery and exploration with less pressure. Your thirties is about exploring your world and goals to the right career (It's "Let's Get Serious Now"), but also time for the 'biological' needs and questions to have or not have a family. Are you going to be committed to having a family with the right person?" In addition, it's the ever-growing need to find the 'right' mate to build a family with for the long haul (Another compounded issue with the years). If that doesn't happen, and you find yourself single in your forties—*Whoa!* Now, the pressure is on to ramp up the efforts both urgently and moved to the top priority slot.

If you remember the show *Thirtysomething,* like I do, man, back then, I thought those guys were so old. Well, imagine what's happening in the mind of the woman or man in their forties—wiser, older and definitely should be targeting on exactly what is desired—right?! Well, unfortunately, the statistics are yelling that the suitable candidates are shrinking, societal pressures are growing, and both external and internal alarm bells are shrieking us hurry up and settle down already. That's right, you are no longer a spring chicken and the dating pool, especially for older women has just signed up for swimming with sharks! Yikes!

Of course, let's not forget the other issue of expectations while dating. All around the world people are dating, but clearly there are differences based on region, culture, and religious expectations. An exception to dating is arranged marriages in the Middle Eastern cultures.

In European cultures, dating is random and frequent—socially enjoying the opportunity of getting to know each other while dating others. There isn't any pressure to commit in this phase of casual dating until both decide to be exclusive. For those people of color, dating expectations varies as their expectations dictate. Religious beliefs also plays a major role in dating and the struggle to find the balance between their spiritual parameters and faith coupled with the acceptable dating practices creates even more stress.

It's clear that finding the right person begins with you being the right person in the first place. Too often we are looking out there, when we should be looking within ourselves to see if we are in fact 'ready' to be a part of a healthy, loving and focused relationship. So, let's briefly look at these dating phases according to Dennis and Jill Franck, in their article entitled "Five Stages of Dating Relationships," they suggest that couples who feel a sense of connection should date for a year or so before getting married. This would afford them an opportunity to see themselves through all seasons. This allows the couples to not only observe, but evaluate each other from coping with different situations, challenges, and emotional circumstances. This would include them dealing with not being around each other, etc. Here are the phases:

1. **Phase 1: Getting to know you** – During this phase, each person is free to date multiple people, without commitment. Significant physical contact will be limited.

2. **Phase 2: Friends with benefits** – During this phase, a couple may have identified one person with whom they decided to engage in significant physical contact. They are still free to out with other people, however, significant physical contact is limited to that one person.

3. **Phase 3: Monogamous Dating** – During this phase, two people have decided that they want to pursue a relationship and end all other dating. During this phase, the foundation of the relationship is stabled, introductions to family takes place, and the beginnings of commitment and accountability are established.

4. **Phase 4: Pre-Marital** – During this phase, the couple will engage in exercises that deepen their level of intimacy.

Communication is key. Expectations are established, goals and drams are discussed, and the future of the relationship becomes visible. Remember, at this phrase, they won't get better on their own.

5. **Phase 5: Marriage** – The commitment is made, roles and responsibilities are established, and the work of the relationship begins.

If you review the information outlined above, you will notice that a pattern will definitely emerge in your personal life too. This is the dating rhythm and most of us have been on this circuit a few times. However, taking it to the next level requires a different focus. One need to be crystal clear on what exactly what we desire and less on what we don't! For this, we need to realize that to find the needle in the haystack of sub-par connections requires us to be what we seek. Statistically, to find that 1:1,000,000 needs a special set of tools that experience, time, and wisdom will make easier to use.

You will note that to have an exemplary, loving, and long-term relationship requires both parties to be fully committed to it. Such is the making of—do I dare I say it?—soul mate are you. Providing the right environment and aligning with vibration for, "Soul Mate" status. Efforts to communicate effectively, trusting the process, understanding, and supporting each other are essential keys to unlocking the challenges ahead.

By building a foundation that is structurally sound, a couple can truly withstand any and most events that could undermine it. You arise from insecurity, mistrust, infidelity, immaturity, emotional withdrawal, anger issues, and/or abuse. Staying flexible with your personal and mutual growth and the changes you'll experience as you both grow into the relationship. Never underestimate the power of patience, time, compassion, and love to help you through those difficult times. Of course, there should always be room for objective professional counseling or guidance from someone who can add value to both of you.

A special note on dating and marriage:

My grandparents, Lebert and Viola Reid, who recently died, had one of the longest union on the planet. We believe this was their first and only that spanned over eighty-years plus. They had ten children and died in their nineties. My Grandmother Viola transitioned on October 30, 2016 at the vibrant age of ninety-nine years. She was months away from being a centennial.

Can I expect that in my lifetime? Maybe not, but it's nice to know it can and does happen.

"Bullshit is the glue that binds us as a nation."
~ George Carlin

Life is not about what others have done to you, but the healthier ideas that you bring to yourself from the experience.

SANDRA'S LIFE GEMS

- Creating healthy relationships will make life more fun and make you feel good about yourself. Nurturing each other to be the best is what an enhancing connection does.

- It is easy to feel overwhelmed and pushed aside when life gets tough and you are faced with stressful situations. That's when a healthy lifelong relationship is key to bringing a fresh perspective and support.

- You know that you have a healthy relationship when it makes you feel good about yourself every time you connect with that person. Unhealthy or just plain bad relationships will make you feel more depressed, angry, stressed or even more vulnerable than you should feel.

- You wouldn't stay on a boat that was sinking? Then why would you continue to be in a relationship that offers the same sinking feeling? In the end, you may feel a slight loss, but you will be glad that you took action in the long run.

CHAPTER 9

PHYSICAL ENVIRONMENT AND FENG SHUI: THE SCIENCE OF GOOD SPACE

Passion is energy. Feel the power that comes
From focusing on what excites you.
~ Oprah Winfrey

Feng Shui, which literally means "wind-water," is the ancient Chinese philosophy developed over 8,000 years ago about the relationships between humans and their environment. This is the art and science of living in the very best harmony with one's natural surroundings instead of disrupting it. Feng Shui practitioners believe that individuals who are in tune with themselves and their environment will see and feel the mental and physical effects. Studies have revealed that the thoughts you have, the words you speak and listen to, the people you surround yourself with and the space all around you have a significant impact on your health, peace of mind and overall well-being.

It's amazing how incredibly different you feel when you slow down your pace and really look around your physical space, from your home to your office space. What's the energy like?

The following guidelines will help you create a more harmonious environment that both invigorates and supports you and the people around you.

How does it work?

A concept commonly used is the idea of a "power" area. In Feng Shui, there are nine power areas inside each room and one of them is the "power position." To calculate your best Feng Shui directions, it's helpful to know your kua number, but it's not mandatory. It's helpful for you to get a better energy facing your best direction. However, with this information you can rearrange your bed. You want to sleep facing your best directions, for instance, the direction the crown of your head is facing in your bedroom. This also goes for your office desk (the direction you face while working), and you will even want to reposition your favorite chair!

The image on this page is a simplified nine-area ancient bagua map that divides any space into nine sections, each of which corresponds to the main areas of life.

You want to direct as much energy into the power areas as possible using the best Feng Shui decorating techniques.

South

WEALTH, PROSPERITY AND SELF-WORTH	FAME, REPUTATION & SOCIAL LIFE	MARRIAGE, RELATIONSHIPS AND PARTNERSHIPS
ELEMENT: WOOD NUMBER: 4 LATE SPRING COLORS: PURPLE, GREEN, GOLD	ELEMENT: FIRE NUMBER: 9 EARLY SUMMER COLORS: RED	ELEMENT: EARTH NUMBER: 2 LATE SUMMER COLORS: PINK, SKIN TONES, EARTH TONES
HEALTH, FAMILY AND COMMUNITY	GOOD FORTUNE CENTER	CHILDREN, CREATIVITY & ENTERTAINMENT
ELEMENT: WOOD NUMBER: 3 EARLY SPRING COLORS: PURPLE, GREEN, GOLD	ELEMENT: EARTH NUMBER: 5 COLORS: YELLOW, EARTH TONES	ELEMENT: METAL NUMBER: 7 EARLY FALL COLORS: WHITE, BRIGHT AND PASTEL COLORS
WISDOM, SELF-KNOWLEDGE AND REST	CAREER, LIFE MISSION & INDIVIDUALITY	HELPFUL PEOPLE, SPIRITUAL LIFE & TRAVEL
ELEMENT: EARTH NUMBER: 8 LATE WINTER, COLORS: BLUE-GREEN	ELEMENT: WATER NUMBER: 1 EARLY WINTER COLORS: DARK BLUE, BLACK	ELEMENT: METAL NUMBER: 6 LATE FALL, COLORS: GRAY, MAUVE

WALL THAT CONTAINS THE MAIN ENTRANCE

North

Activate Your Power Spots

The secret is to choose objects and colors that represent the area in your life you want to improve. Also, pick items that have strong symbolic meaning for you.

Often, the best enhancements are done using something you already have and all you need to do is move them into a power area. Here are some examples of element enhancers:

- **Wood element**: pottery, plants, living flowers, lucky bamboo
- **Earth**: crystals, faceted crystal balls, pottery
- **Fire**: candles, fireplaces, lamps, wood to fuel fire
- **Water**: water fountains, aquariums, waterscapes, paintings, models of boats
- **Metal**: coins, brass or copper trays, statues

Attract More Money Using Feng Shui

The area connected to your financial prosperity and abundance is the southeast area of your home / office. One of the best ways to attract wealth is to place a water fountain in your prosperity area.

Another wealth trigger is pachira, the Chinese plant also called the money tree. The leaves represent the five Feng Shui elements (wood, water, fire, metal, and earth) which make it an ideal living example of harmony and balance of the five elements.

Also, you can place golden objects in your Feng Shui wealth zone, such as coins, to help money flow easily into your life. You can also choose something that is or seems expensive and luxurious and place it in the wealth area as well.

Another great choice is a fish tank. Include goldfish in your tank, as the Chinese characters for the goldfish are a combination of the two characters meaning "gold" and "abundance."

Feng Shui Bedroom Facts and Colors

The best position for your bed is the side of the room diagonally farthest from the door. Also, sleeping in line with the door puts you against too much chi, which can contribute to stress and irritability. Another tip is to never keep your working desk or computer in your bedroom. That's because the two types of energy (work and sleep) are opposite to each other and are incompatible.

The bedroom is usually used for resting so it is considered yin (quiet) energy. Try to use yin colors such as pastel shades and avoid anything too bright and aggressive. The same goes for your bed covers and furniture. You can spice it up a little bit by adding a touch of red—the color of love and desire—such as a red pillow or a bright red candle.

De-clutter and make space in your bedroom, especially if you are looking for a new romantic relationship. Create mental and emotional space so as to enjoy the perfect atmosphere and increased energy. So get out there and start to Feng Shui away.

SANDRA'S LIFE GEMS

- Feng Shui is the ancient Chinese art and science of living in the very best conditions possible. Inside yourself and your surroundings dictate how your energy flows or not.

- In Feng Shui, there are 9 power areas inside each room and one of them is the "power position." Understand how your living and working environment work adds to a more harmonious and peaceful you.

- The secret is to choose objects and colors that represent the area in your life you want to improve. Also, pick items that have strong symbolic meaning for you.

- Feng Shui can enhance your money or wealth sector. One of the best ways to attract wealth is to place a water fountain in your prosperity area.

- Want to create the optimum environment for a new romance? A smart and obvious way: de-clutter and make space in your bedroom. Add a dash of desire by placing a few red pillows on your bed too.

CHAPTER 10

BASIC FITNESS TIPS TO YOU ADDICTED TO STAYING HEALTHY

The only way you can hurt the body is not use it. Inactivity is the killer, and remember, it's never too late.

~ Jack LaLanne, American fitness and nutritional expert and motivational speaker

Did you know that most people choose to go on a diet because they suddenly realize they don't fit into their favorite jeans anymore? I must admit to succumbing to this around the spring and summer months. I know. I'm human too. However we slice it, this is not a good motivator because it makes you focus on what you *don't* want, and that is being overweight.

How about shifting your entire focus to what you *do* desire? To look healthy, trim, and sexy, bursting with energy and vitality and adopting a healthy lifestyle. Putting your health as a top priority each year must be a commitment to see through. I know this is something you can get behind before your behind is too big to care. About a year ago, a friend of mine who was years younger wanted me to join him on a run in Central Park in New York City while I was there. It was just a month into spring and I was about fifteen pounds over my ideal weight. So I thought "Why not?" It was time for me to get more active and just talking about it was getting pretty cheap.

Whoa! That first time, I didn't run more than 200 hundred feet and was absolutely winded! I was very embarrassed and he wasn't helping by the comments he was making either as my coach—he sucked lemons, but I didn't quit. I went around the trail three times that day (though it was the shortened trail) but I was so proud of myself. Like anything in life worth fighting for, I returned with him a few more times and he was brutal on me, but I kept going and then I later went by myself. The result was amazing. I lost sixteen kick-butt pounds and looked amazing. Unfortunately, the winter came and there is was again—ten pounds—so you know what I'll be doing this year as a lifestyle change.

Anyway, here are some simple changes you can apply right now to get more confidence while feeling healthier and more energetic:

✓ **Eat Your Way to Energy**

A good nutritional plan is much more than just weight loss. It's about paying attention to what you're eating and knowing which foods are actually good for you. So start your day with a good breakfast and get the energy you need for the day—at the time when you need it the most. This will help you avoid the afternoon food crash and get the fuel you need to get most things done in the mornings.

Power snacks are great low-sugar protein and fiber intakes that keep you going between each meal. Some suggestions: mixed nuts, nonfat yogurt, peanut butter, frozen berry smoothies, and granola bars.

Also, nutrition experts suggest drinking at least half of your body weight in ounces of water/day (e.g., 150 lbs x .5 = 75oz). This keeps the body fully hydrated and carries the nutrients and oxygen into cells. The brain is made up of 90% water, so drinking enough water helps you think better, be more alert and more focused.

✓ **Balance Your Blood Sugar**

Research studies have revealed that the best foods for optimal weight loss and maintenance are those that don't cause a quick rise in blood sugar levels. Eating smaller, more frequent meals with protein and avoiding sugars helps you burn more fat and keeps your energy and mood more balanced. The key is to eat lots of tasty, low-carbohydrate foods daily. Some of them include almonds, quinoa, millet, hummus, avocado, and walnuts.

✓ **Do a Little Exercise Every Day**

You don't have to lift weights for two hours a day, every day, but it's strongly recommended to do a little bit of exercise at least once a day. What's important here is not the amount; rather, it's the habit of exercising and stretching your body for optimal circulation.

Talking about circulation, I was doing some research and one way that was shared was the concept of staying on your feet and moving around versus sitting. Another thought for those who don't want to go to the gym every day: how about having friends over and mixing it up with a trainer.

Take a look at **Zumba**, which is an aerobic workout that blends choreographed footwork and body movements from salsa, merengue, flamenco and other dances to sculpt your body and burn fat. You'll have so much fun you wouldn't even notice that your toning your abs, thighs, glutes and arms. Or, how about **Hula-hooping**: the fifties craze is no longer for kids these days. It's a great cardio workout to slim your waist, hips and buttocks and thighs while working your lower back muscles and abdominals.

Of course, there's **pole dancing** to get you fit and boost your confidence. **Indoor rock climbing** builds strength and balance and you can burn up to 800 calories an hour. All those muscles will surely get a workout like you would never believe. I tried it, and wow! **Rope Jumping** like when we were kids is still great as an adult. You can burn about 200 calories in fifteen minutes.

Put on the latest music beats and get revved up to burn those calories. How about fencing? It's a fast-paced aerobic workout and if you love to compete this is an extra treat. Interested in

Softball? Check out your local leagues, community centers or join a team or organize one with your friends. Skating is tons of fun and a super substitute for running, especially since it's easier on the joints too. It's aerobic workout at its best and tones your lower body while building leg strength. A 143-pound woman can easily burn about 330 calories during one hour of continuous skating. Look into your local rinks and book some time to get your skating on.

Jack LaLanne used to say, "Exercise is the catalyst. That's what makes everything happen: your digestion, your elimination, your sex life, your skin, hair; everything about you depends on circulation."

For those who might need to get an incentive, look at this short list of activities that will burn calories with a little effort:

- Take public transportation.
- Grocery shopping—Park far away, but in a safely lit area, and walk to and from the store. This will definitely fit more exercise in; the walk and carrying your groceries builds some muscles.
- Housework—Cleaning can really work up a sweat. Hand-wash your dishes and save soap and water too. Vacuum the entire house. Dust regularly. Spend time organizing. Fold laundry standing up and move around.
- Play—Your pets need a workout and kids need a workout too. Play catch or tag with your kids. If you have young dogs, playing catch can get you more exercise with all that moving around. Getting your Frisbee out is just what the doctor ordered
- Walk. Walk. Walk. Use those stairs more instead of the elevators at work. If you watch TV, get on the treadmill and work it too. Look around you and create ways to exercise.

✓ Take Good Care of Your Brain

"Health is wealth" is an old saying. A healthy brain means a healthy mind and a healthy mind means a powerful mind. Playing a game keeps your mind trained (versus watching TV) and refreshed. There are endless options and you can choose anything from memory, problem solving, speed and attention, board or PC games to the more engaging board games such as Monopoly, chess and more. Give yourself the gift of a brighter brain and play.

Your health is counting on you to make the best choices right now! Your health and fitness are calling: are you tuned in?

Now you're on your way to creating a healthier body, mind and life. Eating right and exercising will make you feel better and give you the focus, energy, and motivation to reach your goals.

SANDRA'S LIFE GEMS

- Remember we are all motivated by the same core of fears and desires. Being motivated to live longer and getting stronger in all areas is more important than getting into your favorite jeans through your weight loss efforts, or it should be. Focus only on what you desire and deserve and all your efforts will bring them to you.

- If you hear this once, you will hear it a thousand times—it's all about moderation, from physical exercise to cognitive exercises to diet. Great nutritional and sleeping patterns are necessary and important to keep your body at peak performance. Don't skimp on what's good for you—create a healthy regime and it will always be there when you need it most.

- Eat power snacks that are great low-sugar protein and fiber intakes that keep you going between meals. Eating well means cutting out and some of those fast foods we all love.

- Start using words like monitoring, hold-off, skip, and stretch, and even limiting when it comes to everything you do. It's like saving ten cents of every dollar. In a year, you'll see what a difference it makes.

CHAPTER 11

BUILD CAREERS TO YOUR PASSION, NOT JOBS TO YOUR DEMISE

Choose a job you love and you will never have to work a day in your life.

~ Confucius

Did you know that on average people spend at least one third of their lives at work? It's no wonder then that studies show a person's complete happiness and satisfaction is directly related to the way they view their work.

We usually divide the kind of work we might do into three main categories: jobs, careers, and vocations. Are you living out your calling, or do you just have a job?

What's the Difference?

➢ **Jobs**—A job is only a job, a way of earning a living. You may find good sides to any job, but in most cases, people look forward to breaks, the weekend, vacations and so on.

➢ **Careers**—A career is a step further on people's path to raises, better opportunities and ongoing advancement.

➢ **People** who see their work as a career put a lot of time and effort in their work and usually go the extra mile by working during evenings, weekends, etc. It's no wonder a career is more likely than a job to make you feel your talents are being used and is thus more satisfying.

➢ **Vocation**—A vocation is a calling; it's what you were born to do. It's where your skills, talents and interests come together and give you the power to change the world around you. People who see their work as their vocation are the happiest and get the highest satisfaction from life.

Oftentimes, people who see their work as a calling would do the work for little or no money because the work itself is so rewarding. As Oprah put it, "You know you are on the road to success if you would do your job and not be paid for it."

The Difference Is in the Calling

The meaning of "vocation" is often misunderstood. The word comes from Latin and it means to follow the voice of God or to do what we are called to do. This is the big picture that many people fail to see. Each person is called to be someone and to do things and discovering our mission is a lifelong process of growth and change.

As Frederick Buechner says in his book *Wishful Thinking: A Seeker's ABC*, "The place God calls you is the place where your deep gladness and the world's deep hunger meet." This intersecting point is your calling, your vocation (e.g., the vocation of a doctor might be "healer").

Simply put, a vocation is the answer to *why* you do what you do. Your career can answer to *how* you fulfill that calling, and a job answers *what* you do.

It is never too late to be what you might have been.

~ George Eliot

Time for Introspection

Answer the next questions to gain insights into your situation:

✓ *First, how does your job actually play into your larger career goals?*

    Many jobs can be seen as valuable career steps. But some jobs are not. What do you get from your job beyond the paycheck? This will help you understand what you're willing to give in exchange for that.

✓ *Is your job helping you to move towards your calling?*

    If it does, then stick with it. Use your current job to create a path to your vocation. If it doesn't, then your job is just a way to put some food on the table as you seek a better result.

✓ *Is your career what you were meant to do?*

    You won't believe how many people suddenly realize that their career isn't at all what they want to be doing with their lives. The sooner you know the answer the better, because it gives you the time to start thinking of your job as merely a job rather than a career element.

Look for the Greater Good

You can find a greater meaning in all work, even routine jobs, by considering the greater good the work does. For example, a janitor's work keeps the workplace clean and contributes to greater worker productivity and safety. The salesperson works on helping people find products and services that best match their needs.

Another way to improve your career perspective while feeling mentally great about the process is by doing volunteer work. There are so many opportunities right where you live or work. I remember after graduating from college and exploring opportunities, I volunteered and helped in a telethon at a public television station in New York City. So setting my sights on working at this station, I recall calling the HR department personnel consistently every week for almost thirteen months.

One day in 1994, while expecting my usual response ("Hi, Sandra. No, we have no positions yet for you."), the response was, "Yes, Sandra. We actually have a managing director's assistant's position for you. Would you be interested?" The interview was a success and I worked for a few months when I was given another surprise. I was informed by my new boss that she had been offered the vice president of public affairs position at the prestigious New York Public Library and asked me to join her! Not only was this a prime position (in the heart of New York City's 42nd Street and Fifth Avenue), but I assisted in creating the NYPL's centennial celebrations, which launched a $500 million capital drive.

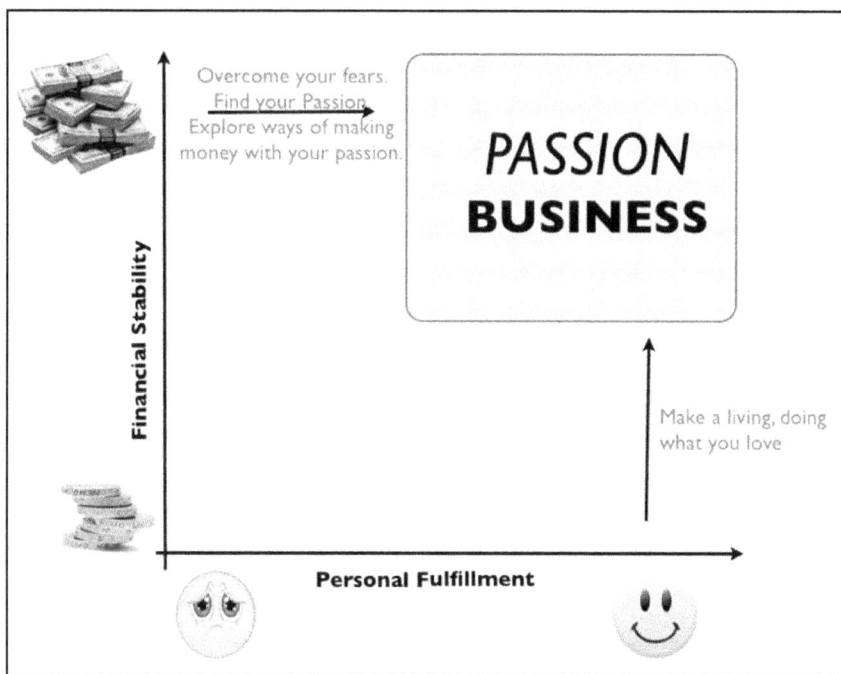

Among other strategic programs, exhibitions and exciting lectures, this position exposed me to some of the top corporate and foundation events, as well as attendees like Barbara Walters and Walter Cronkite, along with many other industry greats.

This just goes to show that from a small choice, a great opportunity awaits. Focusing on the greater good in every job—rather than the daily duties—can provide meaning and a sense of worth from your work. More importantly, keep your dreams and passions firmly planted in a career that excites you because you might just get the opportunity to really shine.

SANDRA'S LIFE GEMS

* We usually perceive our work in three main categories: jobs, careers, and vocations. Are you living out your calling, or do you just have a job? Know the difference.

* This is the big picture that many people fail to see. Each one of us is called to be someone unique. Doing things that help us discover our mission is a lifelong process of growth and change.

* Simply put, vocation is the answer to *why* you do what you do. Career answers *how* you fulfill that calling, and a job answers *what* you do.

* It's important to consistently address self-introspection and to answer the questions that link you from the small to the bigger picture of you being your best in all that you do.

* Unlocking your passions and the activities that create your dreams will align to your inner passions. Be the advocate for what serves you best and the results will create a career worth having for life.

CHAPTER 12

WHERE ARE YOUR FUN & JOY HIDING?

A life without love in it is like a heap of ashes upon a deserted hearth—with the fire dead, the laughter stilled, and the light extinguished.

~ Frank P. Tebbetts

In our fast-moving lives, we miss many moments and we forget a lot. We often need to fight against the constant belief that our worth is dependent on keeping ourselves as busy as possible. Or that the good in life is somewhere in the future when you'll have the right money, the right house, the right spouse ... you know what I mean. Wake up to your *real* life and go after experiences that satisfy your core needs, and let's do some living before we die.

Science says...

...that leisure experiences can increase good moods and self-esteem. Joyous, fulfilling experiences make us happier than material stuff, so the more active you get, the better you feel. You can add a few hours of joy to your forty-hour work week and do something with a lot of passion. It helps you build strong social relationships, increase performance and act as a stress buffer, which is exactly what we need these days.

And there's so much to choose from no matter where you are, who you are, or how much money you have in your pocket. Getting down to your passions and preserving your hobbies can be a tremendous gift you give yourself. Hobbies help you relax and bring about personal fulfillment.

Spinning the Wheel of Life

Create a balanced life by bringing your passions close to your activities. Be willing to break the rules so that you feel more alive. Do things you think of doing and live a life of no regret. There will be plenty of time to contemplate when life flips a page. You will be more focused, directed, and purposeful. You will have the state of mind that creates the life you want.

Eliminate stress by learning to lead a balanced life. To find out how to achieve work and life balance, evaluate your balance with the wheel of life. You will gain valuable feedback on the areas of life that are doing well, as well as those that are lacking.

The wheel has eight segments and each one has concentric circles numbered from 1-10. For each of the eight segments, determine how satisfied you are with that particular area of your life.

Take a look at your results. The ideal wheel of life is perfectly round and large. If you're like most people, the wheel won't come out perfectly round and that is a strong indicator that specific areas in your life are lacking balance.

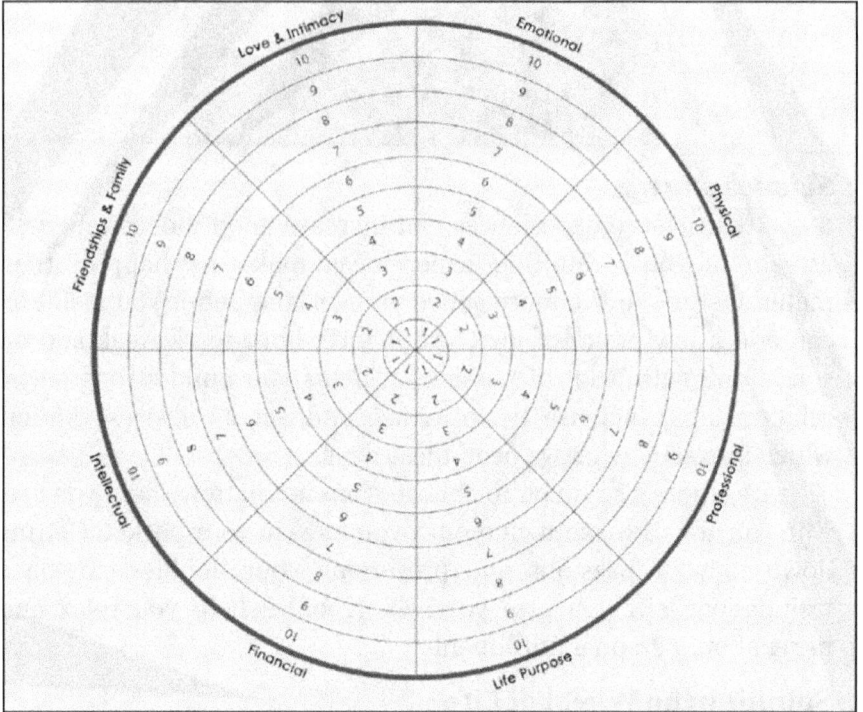

So, try to infuse your passion into your weekly routine and you will feel totally recharged and connected throughout the rest of the week. Get out there and participate in what scientists say makes us happy: dancing, hiking a trail, hang gliding, travelling, and exploring new cultures. Read that book you've been putting off for months, learn that new language to get a promotion or to use in your travels, play an instrument, or fool around the house on a Sunday morning and feel like you're eight again.

Do what you love and try things you've never done before. You'll be amazed by how enriching and simple life really is!

SANDRA'S LIFE GEMS

- We've grown to accept all the excuses and erroneous belief systems. You must fight against the constant belief that our worth is dependent on keeping ourselves as busy as possible. The truth is, there is more to life.

- The goals you are setting will provide clarity and a sense of purpose that are critical to a purposeful life and being happy.

- The wheel of life (used by life coaches everywhere) is an effective tool that helps us eliminate stress and create a more balanced life. Use it and be it.

- The good life is not somewhere out there in the future or when you have the right money, the right house, the right spouse. It's when you decide that you deserve more and will set out creating it.

- Do what you love *now* and everything else will sort itself out. It always does, and that's the amazing thing we need to remember. Always remember that when things are at their darkest.

CHAPTER 13

ROMANCE BASICS 101

To laugh often and love much ... to appreciate beauty, to find the best in others, to give one's self ... this is to have succeeded.

~ Ralph Waldo Emerson

How do you get it right the first time? Want to walk into the sunset forever after with that special person? Let me share with you a few pointers to sink your teeth into right now.

Begin with the End in Mind

I want to remind you of a very powerful success principle that works in any area of your life. It says that you should always begin with the end in mind. Based on how confident, happy, loving and free you are with your S.E.L.F. (Self Elevates Life Forward), you need to be the real *you*. To share outwards, you need to embrace all the wonderful qualities in yourself to share with others. Then, with such a solid and confident

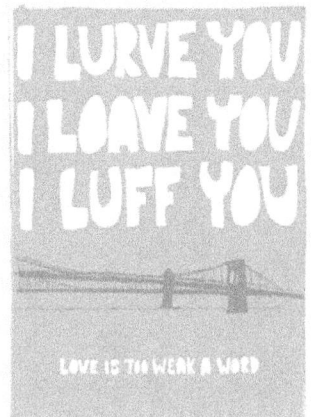

I LURVE YOU
I LOAVE YOU
I LUFF YOU

LOVE IS TOO WEAK A WORD

foundation, you can slowly involve others to share who you truly are.

Whatever you want to accomplish, you start with that, and then work backwards to create the steps needed to reach your goal. You can take this principle and apply it to your love life, and once you understand how it works, everything falls into place.

So before you even begin to search for answers to any of your relationship problems, ask yourself, "What is it that I want to experience in my relationship, what kind of a commitment do I want, what kind of person would best fulfill my needs?" Once you know what you truly desire, you'll have a clear image of the ideal relationship you want for yourself. Because if you don't know what you want, you won't know when you've gotten it.

Solve Conflicts—the Easy Way

One of the most important components in any successful relationship is knowing how to solve conflicts. Most people just ignore the elephant in the room hoping it will eventually go away. Unless you're Houdini, you won't make it go away and you'll just end up in a ton of frustration and repressed anger because of all the unresolved issues.

> ➢ **Acting "As If"**

I found the following exercise to be extremely helpful whenever a situation appears overwhelming. Every time you find yourself in a tough spot, reclaim the loving relationship you want by "acting as if" you and your partner are getting along just fine.

This way, you create the perfect environment to manifest your desires, and as you do, you are sending out a powerful signal that bring your circumstances that match that. If it seems ridiculous, try to communicate as little as possible while gradually restoring peace and harmony. In the end, that's what a romantic relationship is: two individuals who feel enhanced by the relationship with trust, love, fun, support and respect.

> ➢ **Speak the Same Love Language**

Unhappiness in any relationship often has one simple cause: we speak different love languages, believes Dr. Gary Chapman (world famous marriage and family life expert). During his thirty-year long counseling career, he identified five love languages:

- words of affirmation
- quality time
- receiving gifts
- acts of service
- physical touch

Some people want focused attention, others need praise and affirmations; others want gifts, while others see cooking a meal as the supreme proof of their partner's love. Other people find physical touch the greatest sign of affection: holding hands, giving back rubs and sexual contact. Chapman also explains how you can discover your spouse's—and your own—love language by following some very simple steps that you'll find in his "Five Love Languages" series.

Be Honest!

When we have nothing to hide, we have everything to give and gain. Within a loving relationship, you can safely reveal your own truth or feelings and it will become evident to you that hiding the truth limits your ability to love your partner. And when you do that, you can't help but limit yourself, and frustrations follow.

So if you want a healthy relationship or marriage, if you are determined to build a successful union, then this is one piece of advice that you can't afford to ignore.

Always ask yourself:

"What can I do to make my partner's life easier?"

"How can I better demonstrate the love I have for him/her?"

SANDRA'S LIFE GEMS

- True romance is always about sharing while being your best self. The relationship is an enhanced extension of your authentic self at all times. To get it right the first time is great, but learning who you are in the process is priceless.

- "Begin with the end in mind." Habit 2 of Stephen Covey's *Seven Habits of Highly Effective People*. It basically refers to your self-discovery and how to clarify your deeply important character values and life, or in this case, romantic goals. For you to achieve your stated mission, you need to see it.

- The ability to solve conflicts in your life while getting the desired outcome is important, but for a romantic relationship, it is critical. Clearly and honestly stating your feelings and understanding your mate's will eliminate tons of frustration for both parties.

- Get to know your Love Language and discover your mate's. Bottom line: your relationship will need it.

- Always check the temperature of your relationship and find out how you can make each other's life easier while always demonstrating love. What would love do?

CHAPTER 14

CREATING AND MAINTAINING YOUR MONEY NOW USING THE LAW OF ATTRACTION

Concentration is the secret of strength.
~ Ralph Waldo Emerson

A few years back, I read a book by Robert Allen called *Multiple Streams of Income: How to Generate a Lifetime of Unlimited Wealth.* It was a paradigm-shifting book for me, and set me on the road to looking at ways to diversify the ways I could earn.

But let's start at the beginning. First...

Change the Way You Feel about Money

Some people spend huge amounts whether they have the money available or not, while others save compulsively whether they have to or not. The way you think and feel about money is either linked to experiences of wealth or poverty, or the way in which your parents related to money, for instance.

If you're like most people, then you've probably grown up with a lot of limiting beliefs about money: only the rich had it, you had to work hard for money, money doesn't grow on trees, etc. It's no wonder why so many people truly believe that life is difficult and acquiring wealth sounds almost ridiculous.

The amount of prosperity in your life is dependent on whether you feel you deserve it or not. As Louise L. Hay (the American motivational author) put it, "As you can conceive of more, more will come into your life."

So every time you find yourself expressing a negative belief about money (e.g., you see a great car and you say, "I'd have to work all my life to afford such car"), change it with a positive one (e.g., "I'm sure I'll have this car in my life because I'm allowing it to come into my reality").

If you want to become an entrepreneur, for instance, then Robert T. Kiyosaki's book, *Rich Dad Poor Dad,* is a must-read. You cannot enter the world of finances without becoming financially literate first. This book will change the way you think and feel about money, forever.

Choose Your Role Model

Why reinvent the wheel? If someone else has already made it in your area of interest, why not learn from what they've done and use it to your own success? I can't stress enough the importance of having a role model, someone you can look up to and follow in their footsteps. You don't need to become a copycat; just apply the acquired knowledge to whatever your goals are.

Let me share with you a brief event that became a lifetime opportunity for me to cherish and one that encouraged me to dream big and produce bigger with a role model in mind. One day, in New York City, after leaving Lord and Taylor's spa, I crossed Fifth Avenue heading uptown to continue my blissful afternoon. I was slowly walking up to the light that had turned red and couldn't believe my eyes: the tall, handsome, and quite distinguished gentleman standing beside me was none other than Sidney Poitier.

So I jutted my head out and up and he turned towards me—I gasped and swallowed—it was him. Looking straight at him, I just went for it. I said, "Excuse me, Mr. Poitier, I just want you to know how much I respect, admire and appreciate all your works to date." Still only half-believing it was really him, I continued, "I just want you to know that we are forever indebted to you for sharing such classics as *Raisin in the Sun, To Sir, With Love* and everything else you've done to date. You've truly made my day." With his signature and gracious smile he said, "Actually, young lady, it is you who has made my week!" Wow!

The light changed and he said he was catching a cab and he would be delighted to give me a lift. To which I replied, "Thank you so much, but I'm actually going the other way, but I do appreciate the offer." He bid me a good afternoon and I slowly headed the other way. As I walked away, two things came to mind: the first was that I was going the wrong way; I actually *was* going his way, but I felt that that special moment was based on pure respect and appreciation. He had plenty of fans happy to prolong that exchange, but I was honored to meet someone who meant so much and to give him that space. I was humbled by being at the right place and time to experience what I knew all along: he was a true gentleman.

The other thought was that you never forget an experience that profoundly touches you in an appreciative, positive way. Choosing the right role models has a way of reinforcing the right kind of motivations to get you and your goals moving forward.

(Note: In 1974, Sir Sidney Poitier was appointed Knight Commander of the Order of the British Empire (KBE), and in 2009, he received the Presidential Medal of Freedom from President Barack Obama).

Set Goals

Whether you want to start a business from scratch or simply want a better paying job, you need to set goals. Goals give you clarity, keep you on track and allow you to evaluate your progress.

Let me give you one example so you can see how a focused mind really works: imagine a room jammed with people wearing all kinds of colors. Now look around and identify anything that has the color blue. You will immediately spot anything blue, even the items you haven't noticed before.

This is the power of focus, the ability to zoom in on something that's important to you. Just as a magnifying glass can focus sun rays on a specific point, so can you focus your life on your mission statement and purpose.

Failure Is Feedback

Getting back to Robert Allan's book, *Multiple Streams of Income*, there is a great idea that I want to share with you. He says that successful people see failure as valuable feedback. So in order to acquire any level of financial wealth, you need to learn to conquer your fear of failure. No matter how big or unthinkable your goal is, you can break it into baby steps that you can take one at a time.

"Don't look at the immensity of the goal. Just keep your eyes on the next step," Allen says in his book. Think of your mistakes as stepping stones to success that give you confidence, which turns into valuable experience. And experience, Allen says, will keep you away from fear. And when you do that, you have the world at your feet.

Hopefully, these ideas have made you see the world outside your limiting box of ideas and for you to finally remove the barriers that stand between you and your dreams. Yes, your dreams! Remember: "A journey of a thousand miles begins with a single step."

Just take the first step and every new move—good or bad—turns into experiences that will ultimately make you fearless and propel you on the top of the mountain. A height you will know instead of being only a dream for you.

In conclusion, if you really desire wealth in all its forms, then you must be what you seek within. Share freely who you are without concerns of how, where or why and it will freely return to you – trust me: it works!

SANDRA'S LIFE GEMS

- Creating and maintaining your money now using the law of attraction is understanding that all focused energy generates either abundance or lack in your life. So if you want to see which you are generating, look at your present "money" sector. Is it characterized by plenty or scarcity?

- Change the way you think or feel about money. If you continue to tell stories of shortage on a continuous basis, the universe only hears the lack and returns it to you. You will be on a perpetual cycle of lack, and every facet you think you don't have or need will always be lacking. Change the outcome by changing the focus. You do have enough, and by saying, being and acting as such it will prove true.

- Find a role model whose life resonates with yours. What were the financial challenges they faced and how did they go about resolving them? What series of actions helped them come to the other side of wealth in your view? Repeating similar affirmations in your life and actively changing from your negative attitude and toxic programming will make your desires more abundant, which, in turn, attracts more people, events and opportunities which will align with your financial goals.

- I can't stress enough the value of positive thinking, exploring and learning about great habits of abundance in your life. Think of things already happening and enjoying the fruits already. It's those conditions that are critical to manifesting all your desires. I know initially it will feel like a ridiculous tale or you will feel like you are lying to yourself, but think about this for a minute: When you go to bed, do you ever question that the sun will never rise? Or that it would not set in the evening? No. Why not? Only by expecting the best will you most likely get it. Don't be a

Chicken Little—Always expecting a crisis in any moment. Instead have that feeling that you will receive the windfall you know you deserve or to meet your financial goals through persistent actions and faith that it will move you forward and manifest, too.

Reading about industry leaders who have repeatedly lost and regained mega-dollar deals, their homes, or lived in their cars will give us all a boost and true perspective on wealth building. These folks never quit, and their failures collectively made them stronger than even they thought they'd be. How strong would you be under those circumstances? The truth is you can do the same—go for it!

What really do you have to lose—Fear? Insecurity? More importantly, what do you stand to gain? How about confidence, security and control instead. Isn't it time to take a risk and choose to now know? Do you remember, in the movie, *The Matrix*, the lead character, Neo, had to make a life-changing choice? This was one of those pinnacle moments in the movie. The nail-biting moment shows he could either stay in the dark and take "The Blue Pill" and be safe, or dare to find out what was on the other side of the Matrix and take "The Red Pill." So, what pill will you choose? "The Known?" Or, like Neo, will you choose "The Unknown?" It's time for you to choose your destiny and know YOUR GREATEST SELF is yet to be created by you!

CHAPTER 15

STRESS—CUT THE BULLSHIT OUT

Dear Self,

Don't get worked up over things you can't change, people you can't change. It's not worth the anger build up or the headache. Control only what you can. Let go.

~ Love, Self

KEEP CALM AND DON'T STRESS

There is a saying, "Most stress is caused by three things: Family, Money & Family with no money." Admit it that is funny, but can be quite true. Seriously, if you live on this planet and haven't experienced some level of stress at some point in your life, give me a call. For the rest of us, we'd like to find ways to keep most forms of stress at bay. So, this begs to ask what the heck is stress and why are we doing our best to deal with it?

What is Stress?

I thought you'd never ask. Well, according to The American Institute of Stress (AIS), "Stress is not a useful term for scientists because it is such a highly subjective phenomenon that it defies definition. And if you can't define stress, how can you possibly measure it?" So, while everyone can't quite agree on a universal definition of Stress, it appears all of the AIS experiments & clinical research appears to confirm that "...the sense of having little or no control is always distressful – and that's what stress is all about."

What Role Does Stress Play in Our Lives?

Believe it or not, most people will be affected by stress in most facets of their lives in varying levels. So, here comes a question that will put stress in perspective. If I ask ten people in a room, "What are the five (5) most important things in your life? Time's up. What was your answer? Okay, let's see if you are right. The research shows that: Money, career (work), relationships, family and financial or economic stability. Now, how many of these affect your life and causes you sleepless nights—hence, stress?

Well, the American Psychological Association in 2010 did a research and found these five factors are the reasons Americans find themselves stressed the heck out! No, you are definitely not alone.

Talking about the impact stress has on your world; let's focus a little on relationships, dating and heartbreak when they fail. Yep! Heartbreak can cause major stress. Not only is it painful, but a broken heart syndrome known as Takotsubo cardiomyopathy occurs when the bottom part of the heart grows in a shape of a balloon or like a potted plant. This is caused by extreme stress or grief; the stress hormones overflow the heart and the body response accordingly.

Keeping your body healthy should be a top priority and even with the thought of a loving relationship gone sour, you need to truly limit the wear on tear of your ticker. Seriously, no bullshit here: as you become more mature and wiser, it is critical to streamline who you croon for these days. Too much effort on an unworthy individual can cost you more than a sleepless night or two.

It is parallel to marrying for all the wrong and regrettable reasons from "Not wanting to let your family down" or "Tired of the dating scene" to "Marrying because the other has money and security," period. Even for this example, is being perceived a "Gold-Digger" worth the headache? Make sure the person you pine for is worth risking it being broken in the long run. The worse thing is to weaken it for an even weaker soul. Did you get that? Good.

"A survey suggests that around three-fourths of the overall human population undergoes stress at different levels in a period of two weeks. It is more common in working populations who are particularly subjected to mental, physical, and emotional stress."

~Excerpt from "American Psychological Association—Stress in America: Our Health at Risk," which shows that there is much more to being stressed out over a period of time.

Stress can create such trauma in the short-term, but over longer periods it can create even greater damages – so be forewarned. Next time you feel stressed, think of how much you might be causing physical damages to the body from sleeping disorders, Post-Traumatic Stress Disorders, increases the risk of hypertension, compromising immune systems, cardiac disease, and inflammatory disease and in some cases cancer.

Did you know? High cholesterol, chest pains, depression, and cardiac problems are mostly caused by stress? It is considered one of the main factors that can stimulate an initial dis-ease into a full-blown attack or life threatening disease. Are you still thinking you can afford to handle stress? I hope you are getting the picture how lethal it can be.

Now, some good news...

Well, now that you see the damages that can be caused by stress, it's important that we create a balanced picture here too. Even if you won $50,000,000 in the lotto – Yes, that would be nice. However, do understand this would still be considered stress. Ah! Good one to have, but still stressful to deal with if ill prepared. So, here's some good news one of many simple ways to cope with any kind of stress in general. Before you can change, eliminate, and embrace a healthier lifestyle from stress, you need to be honest what you can and cannot control. By understanding your genetic, lifestyle choices, career aspirations, and behavior you are in the best position to do more or less about the role of stress in your life. It is imperative that you start making better choices for your health and well-being before you no longer have a choice to make.

By now, you are wondering what options are available for you to stay on a track to better living. Well, believe it or not it will cost you something to permanently change bad habits or choices to stress-free ones. It will start with your wanting to change for the right reasons. In addition, the core thought for all things in life, begins and ends with your choices for it. Make no mistake, the more kindness, compassion and love you demonstrate inwardly MUST radiate outwardly.

One key ingredient to your success is the strength of your self-discipline required to implement positive thoughts and change behaviors to effectively improve your overall life. Moving away from the obvious or subtle "Emotional Vampires" or destructive patterns you've cultivated over the years will once and for all free you to be the real "Stress-Free – No Bullshit" YOU. Will it cost you a bundle?

The answer begins with a resounding: Yes. The bundle required is a dash of honesty, a sprinkle of compassion, a sprig of love and a bucket of laughter—not in any particular order. Repeat this dosage daily until you find yourself achieving the emotions that create more of the same despite the waves of issues around you. You can beat the crap out of stress by virtually laughing your way to good health.

You know the thought of always looking for "The Sunny Side of Life" from the classic Monty Python's series. Pretty soon you will agree with Dr. Wayne W Dyer: "Positive thoughts keep you in harmony with the universe," especially inside you. Did you know that chewing some gum now and again is considered quite the elixir for dealing with stress? You see, chewing gum lowers the stress level, which is known by the ancient Greeks and Mayans that chomping on resin gums are relaxing, too.

If trying all these methods still won't get you to the "Serenity Within," then maybe it's time to just shut-down and switch off to find that inner-harmony. It's amazing when you just let go and let good silence in for fifteen to thirty minutes to get you mind, body, and spirit grounded. Meditation is really just zoning out and focusing on a singular object or thought that stimulates the happiness within. Too many times, we all are looking for that perfect moment, opportunity to make it happen.

I was listening to an audio of the famous Thích Nhất Hạnh, a Vietnamese Buddhist monk, teacher, author, poet and peace activist who now lives in southwest France where he was in exile for many years. He was sharing his thoughts on the "Practice of Mindfulness" in my car one day. It was a very soothing and welcomed change from all the blaring music, talk personalities, and advertisements blasting through the different radio stations.

One thought that stuck out was his ideas as it related to one's "Awareness of Now" and likened it to the traffic light we all would patiently or impatiently wait to change. Paying attention to when the light changes and that specific focus required an acute awareness. Seeking inner-peace and solitude in a world of chaos can be a challenged, but if we don't balance our lives—it will surely unbalance us—*Right*?! Take time to breathe, think, and find peace.

Finally, since most of us will find ourselves in and out of given relationships it is important to understand how accepting others and how we relate to each other's quirks organically will make all the difference. You must understand your limitations and avoid bringing stress and all its relatives (emotions that trigger overall fear, pain, anger and helplessness) into your own world. Be more open to be closed to certain habits from yourself or others that introduces you to your worse self. Dating in general can be stressful if you approach it without the proper attitude and expectations. Your goals and the process should not make you feel "Trapped" in any scenario. You do have a choice with every step you take and make.

Look to your past as a guide to where you can be if you continue to do the same things over and over. It's the dawning of a new day and a new you. Keep reaching for that better, healthier side by eliminating the untruthful, bullshit diet that brings less to the table. You are more than you were then and much more than your future can fathom.

Our greatest weapon against stress is our ability to choose one thought over another.
~William James

SANDRA'S LIFE GEMS

- Worry less about all that is happening in and around you. Stay open to your truth and your honest thoughts of changing outcome will shine through. Worrying ONLY brings more frustrations, bags under your eyes and most likely adds other unhealthy habits. Simply cut it out!

- Change how you look at stress by changing how you deal with it in all its forms. You can and will overcome whatever you are dealing with as long as you have another breath in you – Just breathe. Let it out and let the stress go.

- When is the last time you said "Screw it" and changed the outcome to get more satisfaction in the end? Seriously, sometimes you just have to move in for more hugs, more laughs, and more fun in your life. The rollercoaster will always be there with one less passenger for a while. Free up some 'You Time' and get some passion back in there. Remember, you are the creator of your destiny. The sooner you know this is the sooner the outcome will be yours.

- The Biggest Bull is not calling it Bullshit! I know it might be a turn off to state the obvious whether to yourself or others, but you know it is not true. Not only playing this charade is draining, but the stress to continue to do the same thing becomes very unhealthy to all involved. Not being able to tell-it-as-it-really-is is destroying the very fabric of growth, health and happiness. Knowing this, why do you still put up with it! By calling things as you see it will not only lighten your mental load and stress, but free you to be you. To not do so is simply—You got it—Bullshit!

Simply Slow Down! Where's the fire? It's not always wise to squeeze so much in your daily life. Choose wisely how you spend your time and with who? There are only 24-Hours in every day and you continuously testing the Speed of Light will only leave you more tired, drained, and stressed the heck out. Stop doing that my friend. It's time to Live, Laugh, and Love yourself again. Go on...We'll wait.

FINAL WORDS OF WISDOM

Reach your goal,
get the lifestyle results worth having.

"Lifestyle" implies that there is more than one model of "the good life" and that all we have to do is choose. This may be relativistic or self-centered, but we live in an era of individuality, and choosing a lifestyle is a crucial component of defining who we are.

Today, "lifestyle" has special currency among young people, who use it to describe what they like, what they believe, and what they want to do. It's a catchall term. Instead of talking about how they eat, what they do for exercise, or how much they work, they talk about their lifestyle as a whole. All the various facets, instead of being examined individually, are subsumed into the larger lifestyle context. It's no longer a question of what I want for a career or where I want to live or what I do for fun – that's just a subset of the larger question: What lifestyle do I want to make for myself?

What's the tangible benefit? Something we can see, hear, feel or otherwise quantify? We have little patience for "ifs" and "buts" or excuses. Forget about nuances, niceties, or shades of gray. We don't care about the process. We care about results.

Knowing your lifestyle, or finding yourself, is an enlightening experience, not a fearful one. You become self-sufficient and easily do things for others without expectation of something in return. You just know deep down that things will turn out just right for you. You are no longer needy, and you become totally appreciative of all of the things people have done for you in the past. Finding yourself is a time of harmony because you develop that philosophy or belief system that will carry you throughout the rest of your life. When you love yourself and who you are, you will take pleasure in both life's pains and pleasures.

How do you know you have found yourself? When you are able to master who you are and help others to do the same. Creating yourself is not easy. If you have never felt connected to who you are, one reason is you haven't been listening to YOU. It's hard to when you've been listening to so many others in your life. The first things you need to do are breakaway and listen to that inner-voice more often. Of course, the first step is always the hardest, but after that hill, it will be smooth sailing to discovering who you are. Make a goal for something you believe in and want to achieve: be in a play, bowl a perfect game, find your one true love, or even just brighten someone's day.

The reality of life is whatever you decide it should be. Start forging ahead in a different way that is more focused on the person you see yourself as and who you would like to be. Some people won't be prepared to see you in a different or more open light. Yet it's important to forget about what everyone else thinks because you *cannot please everyone.* And while you might not want to disappoint the people close to you, they should want you to be happy as you will wish for them, too. As long as you continue to exist to fulfill other people's ideas of who you should be, you'll never know your true talents, a notion aptly summed up by Raymond Hull, who said: "He who trims himself to suit everyone will soon whittle himself away."

I would be doing a disservice if I didn't remind you of one of the most powerful thought techniques that propel all your hard and smart work in this book to manifest in your life even faster. It's the thought of being grateful and those feelings of appreciation in all your moments. Why? They help you to be in the present by noticing what you do have and stopping to appreciate it. This can be as basic as food in the pantry, shelter from the pouring rain to possessing a car or having parents who truly love you.

The benefits that both these concepts bring into your life are the key to lasting joy and a sense of inner peace in whatever situation you find yourself. Being grateful has the power of changing your mood almost instantly from negative to positive. Good feelings and positive energy come when you start realizing what you are grateful for and all the positive things showing up in your world. They say how being grateful generates good vibrations—it's true. It is referred to in quantum physics as positive thinking, a state that vibrates from your thoughts and it affects and modifies the reality around you. It is said that the first seventeen seconds of any thought are the most powerful, and they can create enough energy to start attracting what you are thinking of into your life. So make your thoughts positive, powerful and sincere. However, be careful what you ask for, because you might just get it.

More importantly, by being in the state of gratefulness, you will stay in the right lane and guard against your negative feelings. Ultimately, this book was created to help you create the inner-dialogue of what true and complete happiness means to YOU. As you mature, you must push your thoughts and actions into higher gears of living. Always remain grateful for each challenging or rewarding step on life process rung. In the end, when adversity raises its head, think of how dire the situation could have been and then raise your thoughts to how grateful you are it is not! Remember that all things are temporary and by being grateful you are making it so. Make this one of your positive habits as you continue to understand the importance of being grateful.

Now, write a list of at least ten things you are grateful for at the end of your day. <u>Remember: ACTION</u> creates Forward <u>Movements</u>.

☛ _____

☛ _____

☛ _____

☛ _____

☛ _____

☛ _____

☛ _____

☛ _____

☛ _____

☛ _____

THE DIAMOND RULES I LIVE BY

> *True friends are like diamonds, precious and rare. False friends are like leaves, found everywhere.*
> ~ Unknown

A STRONG WOMAN VS. A WOMAN OF STRENGTH

A strong woman works out every day to keep her body in fine shape...
but a woman of strength builds relationships to keep her soul in shape.
A strong woman isn't afraid of anything...
but a woman of strength shows courage in the midst of fear.
A strong woman won't let anyone get the best of her...
but a woman of strength gives the best of herself to everyone.
A strong woman makes mistakes and avoids the same in the future...
but a woman of strength realizes life's mistakes can also be unexpected blessings and capitalizes on them.
A strong woman wears a look of confidence on her face...
but a woman of strength wears grace.
A strong woman has faith that she is strong enough for the journey...
but a woman of strength has faith that it is in the journey that she will become strong.
—Author Unknown

KEYS TO BECOMING A WOMAN WITH BALLS

To be a savvy professional woman in today's demanding world takes focus, diligence and a desire to reduce or eliminate obstacles that may hamper our true happiness, goals or life's purpose. It's imperative to create a lifestyle plan that at its very core remains solid against the most challenging life events. Ultimately, you will identify a mastered S.E.L.F. that will slowly and confidently create a woman that defines her roles, instead of allowing her roles to define her! This concentrated effort and grit can only be described as being "a woman with balls" when it comes to going after one's dreams and desires. I deem myself such a woman and I have turned my balls into real life gems. Below are some of these very concepts that once incorporated into your life, like mine, it will be a force to be reckoned with in any situation.

- Clear your clutter and organize your life
- Become a problem and drama-free zone
- Create financial security
- Get on the path to financial independence
- Find the work/career you love
- Attract the man/woman of your dreams
- Get your emotional needs met

- Identify your core values and passions
- Practice amazing self-care, self-awareness, self-love, self-acceptance, self-management, self-reliance, and the all-empowering self-respect
- Read More. Research More. Relax More.
- Eliminate all the petty annoyances
- Make big requests that people respond to
- Communicate with power, grace and style
- Become naturally motivated
- Eliminate unhealthy habits
- Stop doing what you think you should do and start doing what you really want
- Find balance
- Become more playful and fun to be around
- Do what you love with the people you love
- Learn to attract what you want instead of striving and struggling
- Find your personal path
- Design the ideal life
- Have more fun!

https://tateworks.com

MY FAVORITE QUOTES

I have been a life-long collector of motivational quotes. I can't recall a day without cherishing a gem or two that perfectly captured my mood, thoughts or problems. Quotes have the power to positively impact my moment, help me to see things more clearly and motivate me to reach higher levels of understanding within and around me – True Self Mastery. It is with this thought that I share some of my best quotes that succinctly capture the true essence of an emotion or insight that will make me or you feel better by reading or sharing them. Maybe, like me, you can add them to your list, especially on those rainy, thoughtful days.

Remember:
Positive thoughts generate positive feelings
and attract positive life experiences.

Wealth is great, but inspiring others to feel, Do, and be the same: priceless

A man is but a product of his thoughts. What he thinks, he becomes.

~ Mahatma Gandhi

The significant problems we face cannot be solved at the level of thinking that created them.

~ Albert Einstein

Believe in yourself and all that you are. Know that there is something inside you that is greater than any obstacle.

~ Christian D. Larson

Never change your originality for the sake of others. Because no one can play your role better than you. So be yourself. You are the best.

~ Unknown

Before you start to judge me, step into my shoes and walk the life I'm living and if you get as far as I am, just maybe you will see how strong I really am."

~ Unknown Source

My life is my message.

~ Mahatma Gandhi

Falling down is how we grow. Staying down is how we die.

~ Brian Vaszily

It is not what we take up, but what we give up, that makes us rich.

~ Henry Ward Beecher

He who cannot forgive others destroys a bridge over which he himself must pass.

~ George Herbert

It takes courage to grow up and turn out to be who you really are.

~ e.e. cummings

You can have anything you want if you are willing to give up the belief that you can't have it.

~ Robert Anthony

The true measure of an individual is how he treats a person who can do him absolutely no good.

~ Ann Landers

This above all, to thine own self be true.

~ Shakespeare

It is never too late to be what you might have been.

~ George Eliot

The creation of a thousand forests is in one acorn.

~ Ralph Waldo Emerson

Say what you want to say when you have the feeling and the chance. My greatest regrets are the things I did not do, the opportunities missed and the things unsaid.

~ Jim Keller

Inspirations never go in for long engagements; they demand immediate marriage to action.

~ Brendan Francis

If we listened to our intellect, we'd never have a love affair. We'd never have a friendship. We'd never go into business, because we'd be too cynical. Well, that's nonsense. You've got to jump off cliffs all the time and build your wings on the way down.

~ Annie Dillard

The price of anything is the amount of life you exchange for it.

~ Henry David Thoreau

Action is the antidote to despair.

~ Joan Baez

The world itself is a great teacher, a constant guide and inspiration. That is the reason why man is surrounded and sustained by the world.

~ Sathya Baba

Talk doesn't cook rice.

~ Chinese Proverb

Do it, and then you will feel motivated to do it.

~ Zig Ziglar

The past has no power over the present moment.

~ Eckhart Tolle

The only people with whom you should try to get even are those who have helped you.

~ John E. Southard

Don't ask what the world needs. Ask what makes you come alive, and go do it. Because what the world needs are people who have come alive.

~ Howard Thurman

Never apologize for what you feel and what you don't feel, that's a betrayal of your truth.

~ Lessons Learned in Life

There is a huge amount of freedom that comes to you when you take nothing personally.

~ Don Miguel Ruiz

We are so often caught up in our destination that we forget to appreciate the journey, especially the goodness of the people we meet on the way. Appreciation is a wonderful feeling, don't overlook it.

~ Unknown Source

Life is too short to be anything but happy. So kiss slowly, love deeply, forgive quickly. Take chances and never have regrets. Forget the past, but remember what it taught you.

~ Lessons Learned in Life

Ability may get you to the top, but it takes character to keep you there.

~ John Wooden

How does one become a butterfly? You must want to fly so much that you are willing to give up being a caterpillar.

~ Trina Paulus

People become really quite remarkable when they start thinking that they can do things. When they believe in themselves they have the first secret of success.

~ Norman Vincent Peale

In times like these it helps to recall there have always been times like these.

~ Paul Harvey

Every day above ground is a good day.

~ *Scarface*

Positive anything is better than negative thinking.

~ Elbert Hubbard

And in the end, it's not the years in your life that count. It's the life in your years.

~ Abraham Lincoln

When one door closes, another opens; but we often look so long and so regretfully upon the closed door that we do not see the one which has opened for us.

~ Alexander Graham Bell

Your time is limited, so don't waste it living someone else's life. Don't be trapped by dogma — which is living with the results of other people's thinking. Don't let the noise of others' opinions drown out your own inner voice. And most importantly, have the courage to follow your heart and intuition. They somehow already know what you truly want to become. Everything else is secondary.

~ Steve Jobs

Act as if what you do makes a difference. It does.

~ William James

There's no next time. It's now or never.

~ Celestine Chua

We are not human beings having a spiritual experience. We are spiritual beings having a human experience.

~ Pierre Teilhard de Chardin

Honesty is the first chapter in the book of wisdom.

~ Unknown Source

All great changes are preceded by chaos.

~ Deepak Chopra

Every moment you get is a gift. Spend it on things that matter. Don't spend it by dwelling on unhappy things.

~ Celestine Chua

Adversity introduces a man to himself.

~ Author Unknown

What lies behind us and what lies before us are tiny matters compared to what lies within us.

~ Ralph Waldo Emerson

Everything around us is made up of energy. To attract positive things in your life, start by giving off positive energy.

~ Celestine Chua

Don't go around saying the world owes you a living. The world owes you nothing. It was here first.

~ Mark Twain

There is no education like adversity.

~ Disraeli

The mystery of life is not a problem to be solved but a reality to be experienced.

~ Art Van Der Leeuw

Sometimes even to live is an act of courage.

~ Seneca

Do what you love and the money will follow.

~ Marsha Sinetar

All our dreams can come true—if we have the courage to pursue them.

~ Walt Disney

No matter where you are in life right now, no matter who you are, no matter how old you are – it is never too late to be who you are meant to be.

~ Esther & Jerry Hicks

I challenge you to make your life a masterpiece. I challenge you to join the ranks of those people who live what they teach, who walk their talk.

~ Tony Robbins

You live longer once you realize that any time spent being unhappy is wasted.

~ Ruth E. Renkl

Identify your problems but give your power and energy to solutions.

~ Tony Robbins

Things work out best for those who make the best of how things work out.

~ John Wooden

If you are not willing to risk the usual you will have to settle for the ordinary.

~ Jim Rohn

Be content to act, and leave the talking to others.

~ Baltasa

Too many of us are not living our dreams because we are living our fears.

~ Les Brown

The entrepreneur builds an enterprise; the technician builds a job.

~ Michael Gerber

We read the world wrong and say that it deceives us.

~ Rabindranth Tagore

Pain is inevitable, but misery is optional. We cannot avoid pain, but we can avoid joy.

~ Tim Hansel

Here is the test to find whether your mission on Earth is finished: if you're alive, it isn't.

~ Richard Bach

The greatest advantage of speaking the truth is that you don't have to remember what you said.

~ Anonymous

Change will not come if we wait for some other person or some other time. We are the ones we've been waiting for. We are the change that we seek.

~ Barack Obama

You cannot control what happens to you, but you can control your attitude toward what happens to you, and in that, you will be mastering change rather than allowing it to master you.

~ Sri Ram

Your imagination is your preview of life's coming attractions.

~ Albert Einstein

It is your attitude, not your aptitude, that determines your altitude.

~ Zig Ziglar

Falling down is how we grow. Staying down is how we die.

~ Brian Vaszily

Inspirations never go in for long engagements; they demand immediate marriage to action.

~ Brendan Francis

It is not what we take up, but what we give up, that makes us rich.

~ Henry Ward Beecher

Always be the leading lady in your own life.

~ Audrey Hepburn

You must do the things you think you cannot do.

~ Eleanor Roosevelt

Holding on to anger is like drinking poison and expecting the other person to die.

~ Buddha

I did everything he did but backwards and in high heels.

~ Ginger Rogers

Strong women wear their pain like stilettos; no matter how much it hurts, all you see is the beauty of it.

~ Unknown Source

The woman who follows the crowd will usually go no further than the crowd. The woman who walks alone is likely to find herself in places no one has ever been before.

~ Albert Einstein

Women always try to tame themselves as they get older, but the ones who look best are often a bit wilder.

~ Miuccia Prada

Yesterday is history. Tomorrow is a mystery. Today is a gift, and that's why we call it the present.

~ Eleanor Roosevelt

Be a girl with a mind, a woman with attitude and a lady with class.

~ Unknown

Think you can or think you can't—either way you'll be right.

~ Henry Ford

Whenever you are in conflict with someone, there is one factor that can make the difference between damaging a relationship or deepening it.

~ William James

If you don't like something change it; if you can't change it, change the way you think about it.

~ Mary Engelbreit

Don't let the noise of others opinions drown up your inner voice. Have the courage to follow your own heart and intuition.

~ Steve Jobs

Don't be a woman who needs a man. Be a woman a man needs.

~ Unknown Source

We are what we repeatedly do. Excellence, therefore, is not an act but a habit.

~ Aristotle

I know for sure that what we dwell on is who we become.

~ Oprah Winfrey

What you get by achieving your goals is not as important as what you become by achieving your goals.

~ Goethe

Eliminate the negative. Accentuate the positive.

~ Unknown

Positive thinking will let you do everything better than negative thinking will.

~ Zig Ziglar

Keep away from people who try to belittle your ambitions. Small people always do that, but the really great make you feel that you, too, can become great.

~ Mark Twain

The ladder of success is never crowded at the top.

~ Napoleon Hill

Every thought is a seed. If you plant crab apples, don't count on harvesting Golden Delicious.

~ Bill Meyer

Once you replace negative thoughts with positive ones, you'll start having positive results.

~ Willie Nelson

You are today where your thoughts have brought you. You will be tomorrow where your thoughts take you.

~ Ralph Waldo Emerson

All labor that uplifts humanity has dignity and importance and should be undertaken with painstaking.

~ Martin Luther King, Jr.

The only person you are destined to become is the person you decide to be.

~ Ralph Waldo Emerson

Man is a goal-seeking animal. His life only has meaning if he is reaching out and striving for his goals.

~ Aristotle

There is no education like adversity.

~ Disraeli

We find comfort among those who agree with us, growth among those who don't.

~ Frank A. Clark

The world is not respectable; it is mortal, tormented, confused, deluded forever; but it is shot through with beauty, with love, with glints of courage and laugher, and in these, the spirit blooms.

~ George Santayana

The only thing we have to fear is fear itself.

~ Franklin D. Roosevelt

If you have nothing to be grateful for, check your pulse.

~Author Unknown

The past is over... Forget it. The future holds hope ... Reach for it.

~ Charles R. Swindolt

The pessimist sees difficulty in every opportunity. An optimist sees the opportunity in every difficulty.

~ Winston Churchill

The positive thinker sees the invisible, feels the intangible, and achieves the impossible.

~ Author Unknown

Victory is always possible for the person who refuses to stop fighting.

~ Napoleon Hill

Is life so wretched? Isn't it rather your hands which are too small, your vision which is muddled? You are the one who must grow up.

~ Dag Hammarskjold

Be thankful for what you have; you'll end up having more. If you concentrate on what you don't have, you will never, ever have enough.

~ Oprah Winfrey

We tend to forget that happiness doesn't come as a result of getting something we don't have, but rather of recognizing and appreciating what we do have.

~ Frederick Koenig

The best way to appreciate your job is to imagine yourself without one.

~ Oscar Wilde

Appreciation is a wonderful thing: it makes what is excellent in others belong to us as well.

~ Voltaire

To accept ourselves as we are means to value our imperfections as much as our perfections.

~ Rusty Berkus

Life is full of beauty. Notice it. Notice the bumblebee, the small child, and the smiling faces. Smell the rain, and feel the wind. Live your life to the fullest potential, and fight for your dreams.

~ Ashley Smith

Saying yes to happiness means learning to say no to things and people that stress you out.

~ Thema Davis

The components of anxiety, stress, fear, and anger do not exist independently of you in the world. They simply do not exist in the physical world, even though we talk about them as if they do.

~ Wayne Dyer

It's not stress that kills us; it's our reaction to it.

~ Hans Seyle

Everyone wants the truth but no one wants to be honest.

~ Unknown

My bullshit detector is solar powered.

~ Unknown

Maybe our girlfriends are our soulmates and guys are just people to have fun with.

~ Candace Bushnell, Sex and the City

A busy, vibrant, goal-oriented woman is so much more attractive than a woman who waits around for a man to validate her existence.

~ Mandy Hale

MY FAVORITE AFFIRMATIONS

Affirmations are positive statements you repeat daily to create the desired outcome. We impress the subconscious mind by triggering it to take desired actions and manifest change. These thoughts program the subconscious mind to create success in our interests, deeper purpose, convictions and ultimately improve our true results.

All my thoughts are backed by positive, empowering beliefs.

All of my thoughts are positive and constructive.

All my thoughts are positive, healthy, and abundant.

Because I am a positive person, into my life I attract positive and empowering people.

Because I focus on the positive, I know my life is unfolding as I desire.

Being positive is one of the top priorities in my life and I practice this feeling every day.

By focusing on the positive in all situations, I make my life more empowered.

By focusing on the positive, my life becomes problem-free.

Each and every day I reprogram my mind to focus on the positive in everything.

Every day I modify my thinking so I only practice those thoughts which are positive.

Every positive thought I have is an investment in my future's good fortune.

For each situation I encounter in life, I choose only to see its most positive side.

Good things happen to me every day.

Good things keep on happening to me.

I always choose thoughts which benefit my life.

I always choose to think positively.
I always ensure that my self-talk is supportive and inspiring.
I always find a reason to smile, no matter what's happening around me.

I always focus on the present and the positive wherever I am.

I always provide a positive example for others.
I am happy, successful, and fulfilled.
I am healthy, prosperous and happy.
I am healthy, wealthy and wise.

I am immensely positive in everything I think, do and say.
I am impervious to negative attitudes.
I am in complete control of the thoughts I choose to think.
I am in tune with the good in everything, and this good moves constantly towards me.
I am reprogramming my mind to think only positive thoughts.
I am so happy to be teaching my children the power of positive thinking.

I am too busy thinking positive thoughts to have time to be stressed.

I am totally impervious to the negative attitudes of others.

I am totally in charge of my life.

I approach every task with a smile.

I approach obstacles with a thoughtful, positive mind.

I attract great abundance into my life with my positive thoughts and feelings.

I attract positive and empowering circumstances into my life.

I continue to hold positive thoughts and beliefs about the future.

I control my life by thinking positive thoughts and making positive choices.

I control the pictures, beliefs and feelings that I create in my mind.

I direct my thoughts and feelings towards the outcomes I desire.

I dismiss unwanted thoughts with ease.

I easily dismiss the negative attitudes of others.

I easily see the sun behind every dark cloud.

I ensure that all my words are positive and encouraging.

I ensure that I only project positive vibrations to others.

I fill my mind with thoughts of abundance, prosperity and gratitude.

I fill my mind with positive, peaceful thoughts.

I fix my attention only on the best life has to offer.

I focus my thoughts on the positive in others.

I immediately replace any negative thoughts that enter my mind with positive thinking.

I keep my thoughts and expectancy always on good fortune.

I keep my thoughts only on the positive things I wish to experience.

I keep my thoughts positive, and life brings me positive experiences.

I know all thoughts are affirmations, so I ensure that all mine are positive.

I know that I am always in control of what I choose to think.

I know that I can when I think I can.

I know that keeping a positive attitude is absolutely vital to my success.

I only fill my mind with positive thoughts of health, wealth and true happiness.

I focus my power on finding solutions to even the most difficult problems.

Today I celebrate life because...

I remember the past with fondness and joy.

The power of positive thinking is evident in my accomplishments.

I only allow positive thoughts to remain in my consciousness.

I know that negative emotions are like coffin nails and discard them as they arise.

I know that positive thinking increases my joy and energy.

I let negative people be negative and focus on my own positive thoughts instead.

I listen to the words I use throughout the day and vigilantly edit those which are negative.

I live every day with a positive outlook and a light heart.

I maintain a positive frame of mind in all that I do.

I make sure that all my thinking is in alignment with my desires.

The quality of my life improves with every positive thought I entertain.

There is nothing in the world that I cannot imagine myself doing successfully. With the power of my positive thoughts, I create the abundance I desire in my life.

Everyone deserves to be wealthy, including me.

I am grateful for everything I have achieved.

I allow unlimited prosperity and money to flow to me every day.

I choose to enjoy this moment because it is all I have.

~ Some excerpts from *Affirm Your Life.Blogspot.com*

http://affirmyourlife.blogspot.com/2009/08/positive-thinking-affirmations.html

ABOUT THE AUTHOR

Born in Camberwell, S.E. London, England, Sandra B. Tate grew up in Montego Bay, Jamaica. She attended City and East London College in Great Britain and moved to New York City in 1984. She initially studied business management at the New York Institute of Computer Science and Technology before switching to study communications and psychology at Hunter College in September of 1986. While attending Hunter, Ms. Tate became a SEEK peer mentor and a member of the SEEK Provost Committee.

Shortly after graduating in 1990, Ms. Tate began working as a special assistant to New York State Senator David Paterson. She later held executive assistant positions with the New York Public Library, Toshiba America, Inc. and Ann Taylor. She also worked as an information technology consultant for McKinsey & Co. and Arthur Andersen before moving on to become a technical project leader in the information technology solutions group at Deloitte & Touché, where she performed advanced-level research, planning and testing of new technology and related services. She later performed similar duties at the New York City Administration for Children's Services.

As a life mastery coach aka "The Ballsy Coach," Sandra has developed life-training programs as a certified seminar leader (CSL) that focus on the use of effective communications strategies for promoting top-level project success with critical business clients. Most recently, Sandra has concentrated her highly acclaimed motivational expertise on consulting services for life balance and work-life coaching solutions for corporate HR departments, training managers and employees.

Visit **http://tateworks.com** to learn more about Sandra's S.E.L.F. Wealth programs, additional material and downloadable articles on developing your S.E.L.F. Foundation to be your daring best.

Please contact the author with comments or other queries at:

Email: theballsycoach@tateworks.com

Great women are on a quest for true self identity and expression. Evolving with self-mastery on healthy relationships, work-life balance and overall well-being are essential factors. Ultimately, such a woman creates her role always based on truth while seeking happiness from within.

*~ **Sandra B. Tate***

Sandra B. Tate

A woman fully focused
in a place where she wants to be,
positive outcome within her message
just you wait and see
With all the challenges that she came across
I would like to make this clear
as this inspirational woman guides you
there is nothing for you to fear
Agreeable frankness, alluring appeal
works well with her radiant smile
absorbing all of her dynamic energy
makes it all that worth while
A difficult road to travel
could this possibly be fate
no matter what lies ahead of your life
you can always confide in Sandra B. Tate

Peter Pavlou © 2010

www.ingramcontent.com/pod-product-compliance
Lightning Source LLC
LaVergne TN
LVHW021503080426
835509LV00018B/2378